DANIEL

DISCOVER TOGETHER BIBLE STUDY SERIES

1 Peter: Discovering Encouragement in Troubling Times
1 and 2 Thessalonians: Discovering Hope in a Promised Future
Daniel: Discovering the Courage to Stand for Your Faith
Ecclesiastes: Discovering Meaning in a Meaningless World
Ephesians: Discovering Your Identity and Purpose in Christ
Galatians: Discovering Freedom in Christ Through Daily Practice
Hosea: Discovering God's Fierce Love
Isaiah: Discovering Assurance Through Prophecies About Your Mighty King
James: Discovering God's Delight in a Lived-Out Faith
Luke: Discovering Healing in Jesus' Words to Women
Philippians: Discovering Joy Through Relationship
Proverbs: Discovering Ancient Wisdom for a Postmodern World, Volume 1
Proverbs: Discovering Ancient Wisdom for a Postmodern World, Volume 2
Psalms: Discovering Authentic Worship
Revelation: Discovering Life for Today and Eternity
Ruth: Discovering God's Faithfulness in an Anxious World

Leader's guides are available at www.discovertogetherseries.com

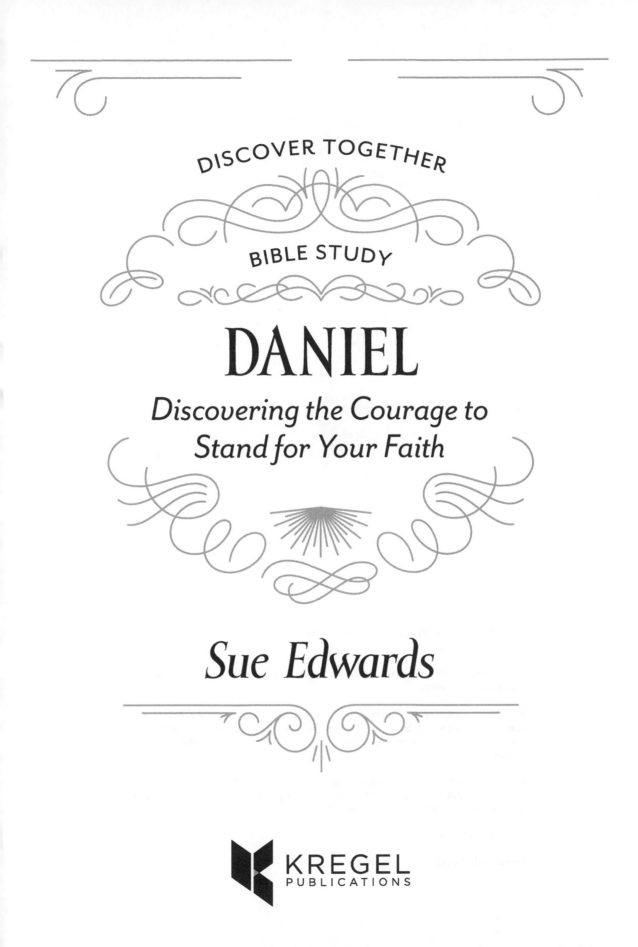

DISCOVER TOGETHER

BIBLE STUDY

DANIEL

Discovering the Courage to Stand for Your Faith

Sue Edwards

KREGEL
PUBLICATIONS

Daniel: Discovering the Courage to Stand for Your Faith
© 2014 by Sue Edwards

Published by Kregel Publications, a division of Kregel Inc., 2450 Oak Industrial Drive NE, Grand Rapids, MI 49505.

ISBN 978-0-8254-4840-9

Printed in the United States of America

Contents

How to Get the Most Out of a Discover Together Bible Study

Women today need Bible study to keep balanced, focused, and Christ-centered in their busy worlds. The tiered questions in *Daniel: Discovering the Courage to Stand for Your Faith* allow you to choose a depth of study that fits your lifestyle, which may even vary from week to week, depending on your schedule.

Just completing the basic questions will require about one and a half hours per lesson, and will provide a basic overview of the text. For busy women, this level offers in-depth Bible study with a minimum time commitment.

"Digging Deeper" questions are for those who want to, and make time to, probe the text even more deeply. Answering these questions may require outside resources such as an atlas, Bible dictionary, or concordance; you may be asked to look up parallel passages for additional insight; or you may be encouraged to investigate the passage using an interlinear Greek-English text or *Vine's Expository Dictionary*. This deeper study will challenge you to learn more about the history, culture, and geography related to the Bible, and to grapple with complex theological issues and differing views. Some with teaching gifts and an interest in advanced academics will enjoy exploring the depths of a passage, and might even find themselves creating outlines and charts and writing essays worthy of seminarians!

This inductive Bible study is designed for both individual and group discovery. You will benefit most if you tackle each week's lesson on your own, and then meet with other women to share insights, struggles, and aha moments. Bible study leaders will find free, downloadable leader's guides for each study, along with general tips for leading small groups, at www.discovertogetherseries.com.

Through short video clips, Sue Edwards shares personal insights to enrich your Bible study experience. You can watch these as you work through each lesson on your own, or your Bible study leader may want your whole study group to view them when you meet together. For ease of individual viewing, a QR code, which you can simply scan with your smartphone, is provided in each lesson. Or you can go to www.discovertogetherseries.com and easily navigate until you find the corresponding video title. Woman-to-woman, these clips are meant to bless, encourage, and challenge you in your daily walk.

Choose a realistic level of Bible study that fits your schedule. You may want to finish the basic questions first, and then "dig deeper" as time permits. Take time to savor the questions, and don't rush through the application. Watch the videos. Read the sidebars for additional insight to enrich the experience. Note the optional passage to memorize and determine if this discipline would be helpful for you. Do not allow yourself to be intimidated by women who have more time or who are gifted differently.

Make your Bible study—whatever level you choose—top priority. Consider spacing your study throughout the week so that you can take time to ponder and meditate on what the Holy Spirit is teaching you. Do not make other appointments during the group Bible study. Ask God to enable you to attend faithfully. Come with an excitement to learn from others and a desire to share yourself and your journey. Give it your best, and God promises to join you on this adventure that can change your life.

Why Study Daniel?

Through the centuries, millions of Christians have read the memoirs of the great Old Testament prophet Daniel and have been blessed in the process. But his words have never been more relevant than they are today. We have much in common with Daniel. No, we weren't kidnapped and taken to a hostile country, never to return home. However, many Christians hardly recognize their now secularized birthplace. We were not taken to a foreign land but, in some ways, our homeland has been taken from us.

Daniel's stories and prophecies inform, encourage, and offer hope as we try to navigate new challenges in a country that has lost its Christian roots. How do we honor God and stay true to our faith in hostile societies? Daniel and his friends show us. That is reason enough to dig into this great Old Testament book, but it's not the only reason.

When chaos and uncertainty shake our security, we need assurance that God is with us, that he cares, and that he exerts ultimate control over the past, present, and future. The book of Daniel declares these truths, providing Christians a firm foundation in sinkhole times. The first half of the book contains six significant events from Daniel's memoirs and the second half includes four visions. The six accounts occurred during Daniel's seventy-year exile while he served his captors as a top government official. These experiences illustrate God's faithfulness during extreme stress and danger. Throughout these hair-raising events, Daniel and his friends honor God and gain pagan favor without compromising their integrity. Lessons we need to learn.

He also describes four indispensible visions that provide keys to prophecies revealed later in the Bible. On a grand scale, these visions paint pictures of God's plan to redeem the world according to God's timetable and sovereign will. They supply the edges of the great puzzle of biblical prophecy. These visions are full of mysterious imagery, making them difficult to interpret, but as we examine them carefully and look for clues in the text, answers emerge that elicit hope in the midst of uncertainty. Portions of the visions have already been fulfilled—the parts that encouraged the Jews as they awaited release from bondage and permission to return home. Other parts of the visions, yet to be fulfilled, serve a similar purpose

Cancer took my father over forty years ago. I have grieved because my husband and children never met him. But three years ago, my husband and I attended a military reunion of sailors who served on a Coast Guard ship in Greece with my father in the '50s. I yearned to connect with anyone who might have known him. The first morning at breakfast I finally found an elderly gentleman who commented, "Yes, I remember your dad. He was a man of great integrity." My heart leapt, as I too recalled the day my dad turned away a bribe of fruits and vegetables left on our doorstep by a Greek vendor who hoped to receive the ship's business. My dad was the supply officer. I'm glad my father cannot see the moral decay that characterizes our nation today. I grieve as I attempt to adjust to the changes around me, but studying Daniel has helped immensely. My prayer is that you will also find comfort and wisdom as you study this man's memoirs. —Sue

for us as we await release from bondage, entangled in godless cultures and pagan bullying.

....

Introduction to Studying Daniel (*9:53 minutes*).

....

Why study Daniel? Because through the dual messages of story and vision, we learn to live, work, thrive, witness, persevere, hope, and bring glory to God in our own pagan exile. Christians today need mentors who have walked these roads and can light the path. Daniel and his friends await.

How to Thrive When You Find Yourself in Exile

Daniel 1

Today, many of us find ourselves in a similar predicament as Daniel and his friends. In 605 B.C. they were kidnapped from their homes in Judah and exiled to Babylon, a powerful pagan nation that did not respect or honor their faith or devotion to the One True God. Babylon worshipped a pantheon of Mesopotamian mythological gods, and Daniel and other exiled Jews were forced to adapt to this strange, unfamiliar situation.

We have not been kidnapped but, just like Daniel, we find ourselves immersed in a culture that no longer respects or honors the Judeo-Christian ideals that once characterized our nation. In a sense, we are also in exile, and our children must grow up in a thoroughly post-Christian world. As a result, many believers are rightly grieving, disappointed, and confused. But others are reacting inappropriately with outrage, hostility, and panic. Do we think that God owes us a place to live in sync with our Christian values? Few Christians have ever enjoyed that privilege, and more Christians are martyred today than at any other time in history. Understandably, adjusting to this dramatic change is difficult.

Does the Bible teach us how to adapt to exile? Absolutely. The book of Daniel is chock-full of lessons to help us exhibit wisdom, strength, and grace in a culture that distorts our beliefs and ridicules our sacred principles. Guided by the Holy Spirit, Daniel crafted his memoirs to prepare us for such a time as this.

HISTORICAL BACKGROUND

Daniel lived at the beginning of what Jesus called *the times of the Gentiles* (Luke 21:24). God offered Israel the role of leading all the nations of the earth, when he told them as he established their nation, "If you fully obey the LORD your God and carefully follow all his commands I give you today, the LORD your God will set you high above all the nations on earth" (Deuteronomy 28:1), but the Jewish nation continued to vacillate between faithfulness and rebellion. He was patient with them for many years, but finally God withdrew his offer and gave world supremacy to

---

OPTIONAL

Memorize 1 Peter 2:23

When they hurled their insults at him, he did not retaliate; when he suffered, he made no threats. Instead, he entrusted himself to him who judges justly.

There has never been a Gentile world power which, as a nation, has had for its *chief aim the glory of God.*
—Irving L. Jensen
(*Ezekiel and Daniel*, 49)

DIGGING DEEPER

In a Bible atlas, locate the ancient nations of Israel and Babylon. How far were the Jews forced to travel as they walked from their homeland to the pagan nation of their captors?

The word *Lord* in Daniel 1:2 is *Adonai* and not LORD *YHWH*. The former word for God emphasizes God's ownership or control, already a hint at a major theme of the book of Daniel.

DIGGING DEEPER

God called the prophet Jeremiah to warn the Jews concerning the devastating consequences of ignoring his warnings. To learn more, read Jeremiah 25. Consult a Bible dictionary to learn more about Babylon, the country God used to discipline his people. What did you learn in your investigation that will enrich your study?

Gentile nations, beginning with Babylon (which is now Turkey, Iran, and Iraq). Since that time, a succession of Gentile nations have ruled the world. We still live in *the times of the Gentiles*, and that epoch will not end until Jesus returns (Luke 21:24–27).

❀ Read Daniel 1:1–21.

Chapter 1 identifies the beginning and end of Daniel's service to several world leaders during the Jewish exile. His service began in 605 B.C., the third year of Judah's king Jehoiakim, and probably ended around the first year of King Cyrus, 539 B.C.

1. Who was ultimately responsible for Israel's defeat and the exile of its people (Daniel 1:2; Jeremiah 27:6–7)?

2. Why had God orchestrated these events (2 Kings 21:1–6, 12–15)?

3. What kind of king was Jehoiakim (2 Kings 23:35–37)?

4. How long did the exile last (Jeremiah 25:11)?

5. What price would Babylon pay for her cruelty and enslavement of Israel (Jeremiah 25:12–13)?

DIGGING DEEPER

Read Jeremiah 51:33–64 to hear the details of Babylon's downfall. What did Jeremiah instruct Seraiah to say and do when he visited Babylon with king Zedekiah? In your opinion, why?

6. From Daniel 1:2, what do you learn about Nebuchadnezzar's attitude toward the God of Israel?

DIGGING DEEPER

If you are interested in learning more about the number and nature of temple "articles" carried off by Nebuchadnezzar and what ultimately happened to them, read Ezra 1:1–11. What is the lesson for us?

7. What do you learn about the outward appearance and inward qualities of Daniel and his three Hebrew friends from this chapter (1:3–4, 17, 20)?

Daniel's gift of understanding visions and dreams was appropriate to his need in a land where such was expected of wise men, and the God who was the source of all knowledge would also give discernment to distinguish the true from the false.
—Joyce G. Baldwin
(*Daniel*, 93)

Hananiah means "Jehovah is gracious," but his Babylonian name *Shadrach* is the name of the Sumerian moon god. *Mishael* in Hebrew literally means "Who is what God is?" implying that the God of the Hebrews was the only true God and above all others. His new name *Meshach* referred to the pagan god Aku. *Azariah* means "The Lord helps" and his Babylonian name *Abednego* means "servant of Nebo," another pagan god. The king's chief official attempted to wipe out the memory of the God of their fathers, but these boys were brought up in homes where God's name was exalted, and it would take much more than a name change to purge them of their strong faith.

Daniel may have had several reasons to resist eating the royal food and wine. First, the food was not kosher. God had given the Israelites strict instructions on what they could and could not consume. Some restrictions were based on health concerns and others reflected theological truths that God wanted to impress upon his people through what they ate. Another reason may be that this food had been offered to idols. This was common practice in ancient pagan religions, and eating or drinking that food implied recognition of these deities.

DIGGING DEEPER

To learn more about Old Testament law regarding food sacrificed to idols, see Exodus 34:15 and Hosea 9:3–4. Why do you think God imposed dietary restrictions on his people?

DIGGING DEEPER

Jesus said that he fulfilled the law (Matthew 5:17) and Paul wrote extensively in the New Testament concerning Jesus' new covenant, which changed the believer's relationship to the law. Write an essay expressing why dietary restrictions have been lifted since Jesus inaugurated the new covenant. Paul's letter to the Galatians and his instructions in 1 Corinthians 8 will help you in your inquiry.

8. What did Nebuchadnezzar have planned for the Hebrew teens who seemed especially gifted, smart, and talented (1:4–5)?

9. Daniel submitted to a name change and to learning about the Babylonian language, literature, mythology, and history, but he balked at eating Babylonian food. Any ideas why (see Ezekiel 4:13; Hosea 9:3–4)?

10. What parts of your culture do you feel comfortable adopting? What parts do you believe God would have you resist and why?

11. Describe Daniel's dilemma (1:8–10). Imagine the conversations between the Hebrew teenagers as they considered what to do. What do you think they talked about and what do you think they did that helped them devise a strategy?

12. What creative alternative does Daniel suggest to their guard (1:11–14)?

13. What do you learn about God's involvement in 1:9?

The most beautiful people we
have known are those who
have known defeat, known
suffering, known struggle,
known loss, and have found
their way out of the depth.
These persons have an ap-
preciation, a sensitivity, and
an understanding of life that
fills them with compassion,
gentleness, and a deep loving
concern. Beautiful people do
not just happen.
                    —Elisabeth Kubler-Ross
                              (*Death*, 93)

14. Consider how Daniel interacted with those in authority over him. What do his actions and attitudes reveal about his character?

15. What resulted from Daniel's suggestion (1:15–16)?

16. Like Daniel, we live in a culture whose values, standards, and behaviors are often contrary to our faith. What enables Christians to stand for what is right in a pagan world?

17. Do you know anyone who has faced a situation where they were pressured to do something against their principles? How did they handle it and what resulted?

18. If you found yourself in Daniel's shoes (for example, if your boss asked you to engage in a transaction that is not technically illegal but could lead to other illegal activity, or if a family member wanted you to accompany her to an event that you find extremely offensive), how do you think you would feel? What do you think you would do? What process would you follow to help you determine a wise response?

Creative Alternatives in Conflict (*6:23 minutes*). How can we model Daniel's wisdom when we need to stand firm in the face of conflict?

19. What did Nebuchadnezzar think of Daniel and his three Hebrew friends after their three-year training (1:18–20)?

20. What do you learn about the character of God as he interacts with his own when they are immersed in a society or culture that does not value his ways (1:2, 9, 17)?

God's people, whether Israel or the church, always stand as the countercultural opponents of the systems of this world. Never was that reality more poignantly lived out than in the Old Testament captivity and exile, and particularly the dominance by Babylon. That national struggle will emerge early in our book, but the first chapter primarily teaches us that righteousness begins with a firm commitment to God.
—Kenneth O. Gangel
(*Daniel*, 14)

21. Daniel, under the inspiration of the Holy Spirit, wrote this chapter to introduce us to his life story. Why do you think he chose this particular incident to kick off his memoir?

22. How might studying this situation in Daniel's life help you the next time you are in conflict with the values, standards, and behaviors of the culture around you? Be specific.

23. What kinds of emotions usually accompany a confrontational situation like the one between Daniel and the king's chief official? Have you ever found yourself in a similar situation? If so, what did you do? What resulted?

24. If you are a parent or grandparent, or if you work with young folk in any capacity, what have you learned from this account to help you prepare future exiled generations to honor God?

25. What does this account teach you about God's involvement in the affairs of the world? How might believing this reality affect the way you respond to your exile, interact with the world, and live your daily life?

Must one point out that from ancient times a decline in courage has been considered the beginning of the end?
—Aleksandr Solzhenitsyn, Harvard Commencement Address, June 8, 1978 (Swindoll, *Tale*, 120)

Lay Down in God's Hands | LESSON 2

Daniel 2 and 7

The second and seventh chapters of Daniel concern two similar dreams experienced fifty years apart. They give us big-picture clues that tell us how world history unfolds and how the world will end. God gave the first dream to Babylonian King Nebuchadnezzar about 602 B.C. and the second dream to Daniel in 553 B.C. These two dreams, although different in form, reveal past and future kingdoms that did and will rule the earth under God's mighty sovereign hand.

When your world spins out of control, these dreams are good news. They assure us that God is still on the throne. He sees, he knows, and he cares. He is wise and powerful enough to orchestrate world affairs toward the end he has ordained. Nothing is out of his reach, although from our perspective, chaos and injustice often seem to triumph. But God is working out his glorious plans despite what we might think. And if God is still sovereign over world affairs and is bringing this world to a beautiful conclusion, we can trust him with our personal concerns.

Sometimes I wonder if I can bear another announcement of bad news, watch another friend suffer, or feel the weight of righteousness slipping away. But when I look deep into these two mysterious dreams, I'm encouraged. I'm praying you will be too.

OPTIONAL

Memorize Proverbs 3:5–6
Trust in the LORD with all your heart and lean not on your own understanding; in all your ways submit to him, and he will make your paths straight.

....

 The Sovereignty of God (*9:17 minutes*). The dreams revealed in Daniel can give us confidence in the sovereignty of God.

....

Scholars disagree as to whether the king had actually forgotten his dream or he was withholding the content of the dream to test his advisers and assure himself that they were accurate in their assessments and not just telling him what he wanted to hear.

At that time in history, absolute monarchs could demand anything from their subjects, and ancient kings were known for their barbaric cruelty. The king's advisers had no reason to doubt the seriousness of the king's threat.

DIGGING DEEPER

Other Old Testament dream accounts show us how God used these nocturnal sightings to reveal his power and to guide events. Study Genesis 41 for another example of how God used dreams to accomplish his will.

 Read Daniel 2.

1. The dream God gave the Babylonian king caused insomnia (2:1). Anxious for relief, he summoned his advisers, made up of magicians, enchanters, sorcerers, and astrologers (2:2). These people communicated with the spirit world and studied the stars to predict the future—practices forbidden in the Old Testament. What unreasonable demand accompanied the king's request for help (2:4–9)? What awaited those who failed or succeeded?

2. How did the king's advisers answer him (2:10–11)? What was the king's response (2:12)?

3. How did Daniel and his friends learn about the king's decree (2:13)? How would you have felt if you had been one of these young Israelites?

4. Can you remember a time when dreaded news caused you extreme concern and stress? If so, how did you feel initially? What did you do? How did the ordeal end? What did you learn?

5. Analyze the way Daniel interacted with Arioch, the commander of the king's guard, and the king in 2:14–16.

> The ability to keep calm under severe shock and pressure, to think quickly and exercise faith in a moment of crisis, these are aspects of prudence and discretion seen in Daniel here.
> —Joyce G. Baldwin
> (*Daniel*, 99)

6. What did Daniel do next? What do we learn from 2:17–18?

> When things are hopeless, pray. When things are darkest, pray. When you have no idea what to do next, pray.
> —Kenneth O. Gangel
> (*Daniel*, 44)

7. What happened during the night (2:19)?

8. Daniel consistently saw God answer prayer. Do you think Daniel enjoyed an unusual relationship with God that resulted in specific answers to his prayers, or does God want all of us to enjoy the same experiences? Discuss.

9. Even in the midst of a crisis, Daniel took time to pray. When a crisis erupts, do you tend to panic or pray first? Why?

10. How many different parts of the prayer in 2:20–23 can you name? How might these elements enrich your personal prayer life?

11. Why do you think Daniel included verse 21 in his prayer? Why is it important that we continue to acknowledge the reality stated in verse 21?

12. Daniel's ability to reveal and interpret the king's dream saved his life and the lives of his friends. Who else was spared as a result (2:24)? What does this action reveal about Daniel's character?

13. What was Daniel's estimate of his own role in the process of revealing and interpreting the king's dream (2:27–30)?

14. Reread Daniel 2:31–38. Who did the head of gold represent? What was the breadth of his power and where did this power come from?

The figure of a man was employed here because God wished to make known what would transpire during man's day, the ages in which mortal man ruled the earth. Here, in one panoramic sweep, the whole history of human civilization is spread before us, from the days of Nebuchadnezzar to the end of time.
—Charles Feinberg
(*Daniel*, 35)

Several features are noteworthy. First, the head is the only member of the body made of only one metal. All the other parts had more than one substance with the exception of the arms. For example, the upper torso was silver but bronze lower down. The same was true of the legs and feet. Second, there is a consistently decreasing value to the substances beginning at the top and proceeding to the bottom of the image. Third, the image was top-heavy. The specific gravity of gold is about 19, silver about 11, brass about 8.5, and iron 7.8. Fourth, the substances progress from the softest to the hardest, top to bottom. The feet are a non-adhering combination of very hard and hard but fragile materials. The clay in view may have been baked clay that the Babylonians used as tiles in construction projects.
—Thomas L. Constable
(*Dr. Constable's Notes on Daniel*)

15. Generally, what did the king see in his dream (2:31–35)? In the chart at the end of the lesson (page 29), draw what the king's dream depicted. (Later, you will compare the king's dream with Daniel's dream fifty years later.) Using the discussion below, label the parts of the statue with the names of the nations they probably represent.

Because Daniel revealed the identity of the head of gold, historians can calculate with some certainty the other nations represented by different parts of the enormous statue. The silver part represents Medo-Persia, the bronze part represents Greece, and the iron and clay parts represent the Roman Empire. Although these parts represented world powers future to Daniel, we have seen them rise and fall. However, in these visions, a fourth nation takes on a form that is still future for us. For this reason, we believe that the center of end-time events will occur in the part of the world where the ancient Roman Empire once existed.

16. In the king's dream, he saw a rock *cut out, but not by human hands* that smashed the statue into such fine dust that it blew away and disappeared (2:34–35). Who is this Rock (1 Peter 2:6–8; Philippians 2:5–11)? What happened to the Rock after the statue disappeared?

DIGGING DEEPER

Reread Daniel 2:44–45. What is Daniel revealing to the king and to us? In what sense did an everlasting kingdom begin during the time of the Roman Empire (Luke 17:20–21)? In what sense will that kingdom be completely realized on earth (Revelation 20:1–6)?

17. Daniel concluded his interpretation of the dream by declaring, "The great God has shown the king what will take place in the future. The dream is true and the interpretation is trustworthy" (Daniel 2:45). How did the king respond (2:46–49)?

18. What have you learned about God from chapter 2?

The second chapter of Daniel has been justly called "the alphabet of prophecy." Whoever wishes to understand the prophetic Scriptures must come to this chapter for the broad outline of God's future program for the nations, for Israel, and for the glorious kingdom of Messiah. This outline is the simple but comprehensive framework of a multitude of future events. No political document can compare with it, and its importance cannot be overstated.
—Charles Feinberg
(*Daniel*, 29)

Note: Daniel's memoirs are not in chronological order. Chapter 7 occurs before the fall of King Belshazzar in chapter 5.

The great sea is probably the Mediterranean Sea (Numbers 34:6–7).

19. During Daniel's twilight years, God gave him an important prophetic dream that he wrote down. What was the setting of the dream (7:2)? Describe the scene.

The first general subject of prophecy in Daniel is humanity in general. He told us how He would direct the affairs of Gentile world powers in the future. He did this by comparing nations to the parts of a man's statue, and to various beasts. What He showed Daniel about Gentile world powers under the man's statue (ch. 2) revealed their *external* manifestations primarily: their relative power and glory. What He showed Daniel about them under the figures of wild animals (chs. 7 and 8) revealed their *internal* character primarily: their haughtiness, brutality, aggressiveness, vileness, etc. Note that these were all wild animals and birds of prey, symbolizing their hostility toward one another.
—Thomas L. Constable
(*Dr. Constable's Notes on Daniel*)

20. Daniel saw four distinct beasts emerge from the sea (7:3–7, 15–17). Describe or draw them on the right side of the chart at the end of the lesson (page 29). Most Bible scholars believe that the four beasts represent the same nations that were identified in the king's dream fifty years earlier. On the chart, label each beast with the name of the nation that reflects this likelihood.

21. What happened to the ten horns of the last beast (7:7–8, 11)? From the description of the "little horn," what can you learn about him?

DIGGING DEEPER

Study the following passages to learn more about this "little horn": 2 Thessalonians 2:3–4; 1 John 2:18; 4:3; Revelation chapters 13 and 19:11–21. Begin to gather "puzzle pieces" to help you put together the end time prophecies in Daniel and other books of the Bible. But remember that you are looking into deep mysteries that are difficult to describe and try not to become frustrated if clarity does not immediately emerge.

22. Who appeared next in Daniel's dream (7:9–10)? Describe him. (See also Isaiah 43:12–13; 57:14–15.)

23. Who appeared after the Ancient of Days (7:13–14, 18)? What happened? What do you learn about their relationship?

24. Daniel asked for help in interpreting his dream, especially concerning the fourth beast, the ten horns, and the little horn. A celestial being explained, in symbolic terms, what will happen in our future in 7:23–27. From these verses, what major events will bring about the culmination of God's plan for the earth?

Although God tells us not to speculate on exactly when Jesus will return, he does hint at how long certain events in his end-times calendar will last. At the end of verse 25, the celestial being told Daniel, "The holy people will be delivered into his hands for a time, times, and half a time." Many scholars believe that this phrase refers to a three-and-a-half-year period of time when the little horn, under satanic influence and enablement, will unleash horrific destruction on the earth. Solid biblical evidence reveals that Christians won't be present for these cataclysmic events, Praise the Lord! This time is called "The Great Tribulation," the last half of the seven-year Tribulation. This period of time is referred to as 1,260 days (three and one-half years) in Revelation 11:3 and 12:6. Tuck away this puzzle piece to help you later in the study as we consider additional hints at God's end-times calendar. —Sue

25. How was Daniel affected by these experiences (7:28)? How do you think you might have felt if you had been Daniel? How are you feeling as you gain hints of what's ahead?

26. Why do you think that God gave Daniel a look into the future? What are the benefits for us?

How will your insights impact how you live today?

27. Giving God control of our individual lives is difficult for most of us. In what areas of your life do you attempt to maintain control? How does this need for control manifest itself? Can you discern why? How might understanding God's control over the affairs of the earth help you relinquish control in your personal life?

Ugh! Giving God control has been a struggle for me most of my life, especially with my husband and children, and now grandchildren. I love them dearly and I want to protect them. But I have learned that God loves them just as much, maybe more, if that is possible. And his long-term perspective and power trump my foolish efforts every time. More and more, I've learned to trust God with their lives and mine, because he alone is all-wise. The by-product has been a calming peace and joy knowing that he really does have the whole world in his hands, and they are good hands.   —Sue

Fill in the left side of the chart by drawing the statue from the king's dream. Fill in the right side of the chart by drawing the beasts from Daniel's dream fifty years later. Label the parts of the statue and the different beasts with the names of the nations they probably represent. Add qualities that you think the descriptions of the beasts might represent.

The Statue in the King's Dream	The Beasts in Daniel's Dream

A Summary of Chapter 8: In our study we will not work through chapter 8 verse by verse, because this chapter parallels what we already learned in this lesson and will learn in future lessons. Chapter 8 does include more detail on the parts of the statue representing Medo-Persia and Greece. And this chapter contains more detail concerning a wicked king who would rise to power during Greece's reign and order the end of sacrifices in the temple in Jerusalem. This occurred in 167 B.C. at the hands of Antichus IV Ephiphanes, who also profaned the Jewish holy place by sacrificing a pig there. But we will learn more about the Antichrist in our final lesson. The bulk of the chapter took place in the second century B.C., revealing prophecies that were future for Daniel, but past for us. If you are a history buff, you will find this chapter interesting. Read it and enjoy.

A Walk in the Fire | LESSON 3

Daniel 3

A curling iron singes your forehead, hot grease splatters into your face from a crackling skillet, you accidentally touch a blistering hot oven. You instinctively jump back because even minor burns sting like crazy. Imagine flames engulfing your clothing and setting your whole body on fire! The very thought makes me shudder. Dictators burn people to scare them into compliance. Interrogators use electricity to pry information from their subjects. In the past, thousands of Christians accepted being burned at the stake rather than forsake their faith. Hebrews 11:34 honors martyrs who "quenched the fury of the flames" with their bodies. These courageous men and women chose an agonizing death rather than denounce the God they adored. Would I be so brave? Would you? Honestly, I doubt any of us can know for sure without actually standing face-to-face with the flames.

Fortunately, most of us won't be asked to sacrifice our life for our faith. But some of us, and even more likely future generations, may pay a high price to worship God. What price do you think you would be willing to pay?

The account we study this week assures us that God is with us when we suffer for his reputation in big ways and small ways, or even unto death. He never promises that he will deliver us *from* our trials but he does promise that he will be with us *in* them. I suspect that Jesus shows up in the midst of terror to soothe and protect his own, resulting in freedom from pain. Whether you are walking through a tiny trial or a fiery one, this passage assures us that God knows, cares, and is right there with us. Daniel chapter 3 paints a beautiful picture of Jesus showing up at the moment we need him.

If you heard this story as a child, familiarity may be your greatest enemy. Pray to see this account through fresh adult eyes. Ask yourself what you can learn about God, about yourself, about the strength required to take a stand for unpopular beliefs in a dangerous world, and about God's faithfulness to his beloved.

The term *Dura* was a common name for a walled off place, often constructed by human hands. Archaeologists have uncovered tall, narrow Babylonian images, similar in shape to the one the king constructed, often made of wood overlaid with gold. The statue probably stood on a wide base for stability.

The Babylonians and the peoples under their control worshipped many gods. This invitation to the dedication was not a summons to worship this idol as the only, or even the most important, god. The king was not asking them to give up worshipping their own national god, only to pay homage to this one too, as a pledge of allegiance to the king. Thus, when the Hebrews refused, the king perceived their rebellion as a personal affront. To him the request seemed perfectly reasonable. In the same way, at times, we Christians are misunderstood in our culture, but regardless we must hold onto our integrity, whatever the cost.

Seven different kinds of government officials were invited to the dedication ceremony, everyone who reported to the king and exercised official influence in the kingdom. This included leaders from the highest rank, listed first, to the least important, listed last, and finally "all the other provincial officials." We don't know how many people attended but probably so many that the king did not notice the three Hebrews who remained standing when the herald demanded that everyone bow down.

DIGGING DEEPER

Read Isaiah 44:6–20. What does God say about idols? Why is worshipping idols so foolish? What does this passage tell you about the king and his enormous golden statue?

We don't know how much time has passed since Daniel interpreted the king's dream, vaulting Daniel to the high post of leader over the key province of the empire and chief adviser to the king.

1. The king made an enormous golden statue of himself (or one of Babylon's gods) and set it up on a plain outside of the city. Look back at 2:31–38 and 44. After hearing Daniel's interpretation of his dream, what do you think might have motivated the king to create this colossal statue?

2. Upon completion of the statue, the king planned a grand dedication ceremony, including an assortment of fine musicians. Whom did he invite (3:3)? Where were they from (3:4)? Why do you think the king desired an oath of loyalty to himself and his kingdom at this time?

3. What did the king require of his guests (3:3–4)? What was the penalty for refusing to participate (3:6)?

4. Evidently the crowd was so vast that the king did not notice three who refused to bow down as instructed. According to Daniel 3:8–12, who were the dissenters? Who pointed them out? Any ideas why?

Where is Daniel during the dedication ceremony? Some scholars speculate that he may have been traveling or that he was ill. Others conclude that because he was the ruler over the entire province of Babylon (2:48–49), he remained at the palace. We don't know for sure, but I tend to agree with those who think he remained behind to oversee the king's affairs back home. One thing we know for certain, he would have joined his three Hebrew friends in the furnace, if he had been there.   —Sue

5. How did the king react (3:13–15)? Who did he challenge besides the three Hebrews?

6. How did the three young men answer the king (3:16–18)? What do you learn about their view of God from their response?

There is no suggestion here or elsewhere in Scripture that the believer will be cushioned against trouble and suffering except by the presence of the Lord with him in it.
—Joyce G. Baldwin
(*Daniel*, 112)

7. Read Exodus 20:1–6, a text the three Hebrew men probably knew by heart and a commandment that undoubtedly influenced their decision to stand their ground a second time. Summarize the verses in your own words.

8. In Exodus 20:5–6, God says: "I, the LORD your God, am a jealous God, punishing the children for the sin of the parents to the third and fourth generation of those who hate me, but showing love to a thousand generations of those who love me and keep my commandments." Since God doesn't hold children responsible for the sins of their parents, what do you think this verse means? In what sense do parents' sins impact their offspring?

9. Enraged, what did the king do (3:19–23)? Imagine and then describe the scene.

The huge kiln would have been nearby to smelt metal for the gold plating and for manufacturing of bricks for the base of the statue. The furnace probably looked like an old-fashioned milk bottle with a large hole at the top for the steam and smoke to escape and a smaller door at the base to shovel in charcoal or wood to feed the fire. Put yourself in the shoes of the three Hebrews. How do you think you might have felt?

10. Why did the king leap to his feet in amazement (3:24–25)? What did he see? What were they doing?

11. Scholars disagree on the identity of the fourth man. Who do you think it might have been?

12. When the king ordered the Hebrews to come out of the furnace, what did he call them besides their Babylonian names (3:26)? Why is this significant?

DIGGING DEEPER

Wring out Psalm 2 in light of the event in Daniel 3. What impresses you about this psalm? Imagine speaking this psalm to the Babylonian king. How might understanding this psalm have helped him?

Was this fourth being Jesus, as many interpreters from the earliest Christian time have suggested? It is impossible to be dogmatic unless one insists that every incarnate appearance of God must be the second person of the Trinity. It is safer to say that what we have here is a reflection of Immanuel, "God with us." God dwelt with the three friends in the midst of the flames to preserve them from harm. In this sense, the Christian cannot help but see a prefigurement of Jesus Christ, who came to dwell in a chaotic world and who even experienced death, not so that we might escape the experience of death but that we might have victory over it.
—Tremper Longman III
(*Daniel*, 112)

13. Who else witnessed the miracle that day (3:27)? How do you think you might have reacted if you had been one of the foreign officials attending the dedication that day? How might this event have spread the reputation of the Hebrew God all over the known world?

14. Daniel includes many details, like what happened to the soldiers, what the Hebrews were wearing, and how they smelled afterwards. Why do you think he included these specifics?

15. How did the king's attitude change that day toward the three Hebrews? Toward God? (3:28–30)

16. Daniel and his three Hebrew friends found themselves exiled in a country where the culture encouraged the worship of many different gods, and making idols of these gods was common. The event in chapter 3 was just one incident in which they needed discernment and courage to know when to go along with the culture and when to resist. What are some of today's idols? (An idol is anything or anyone that takes the place of God in our lives.)

Be careful not to forget the covenant of the LORD your God that he made with you; do not make for yourselves an idol in the form of anything the LORD your God has forbidden. For the LORD your God is a consuming fire, a jealous God.
—Deuteronomy 4:23–24

Prepare for the Flames (*3:45 minutes*). How can we find the courage to stand strong in our own "flames"?

17. How do you decide when to take a stand against a cultural expectation and when to go along with it?

18. What have you observed in the lives of Daniel and his three Hebrew friends that prepared them to live wisely in exile? How can you prepare today to live wisely as an exile in your culture?

19. Share a time when you took a stand against the expectations of the culture in order to honor Christ. What happened and what did you learn?

20. Shadrach, Meshack, and Abednego believed that God was able to do anything, even rescue them from the king's furnace. Do you struggle to trust God completely in situations that look impossible from a human point of view? If so, what situations tend to cause you to doubt?

21. Did the three Hebrews have any assurance that if they were faithful to God then he would rescue them from the flames of the furnace? What assurance can believers count on (Isaiah 43:1–2; Psalm 23:4–6; Matthew 28:20; John 12:26)?

When believers face some white-hot furnace they may be encouraged to be faithful to him confident that their God is Lord of death and that he will demonstrate that he is. The power of paganism offers no ultimate threat. When situations are utterly hopeless, they can trust him to validate their commitment and his power by rescuing them one way or the other.
—John E. Goldingay (*Daniel*, 76)

Therefore, since we are receiving a kingdom that cannot be shaken, let us be thankful, and so worship God acceptably with reverence and awe, for our "God is a consuming fire."
—Hebrews 12:28–29

DIGGING DEEPER

The book of Daniel contains both history and prophecy. Chapter 3 does not contain direct prophecy but it is prophetic in the sense that the king's erecting an idol foreshadows an act by the Antichrist, who during end times will erect an image and order it worshipped. The three Hebrews who resisted typify those who will refuse to worship the Antichrist's image. What details of this future event can you find in 2 Thessalonians 2:3–4, Revelation 13:11–18, and Mark 13:14–23?

When God chooses to use people, he often puts them through difficult, frustrating, and life-threatening experiences to burn the dross from their lives and refine their character.
—Kenneth O. Gangel (*Daniel*, 72)

22. We celebrate the courage of our heroes in Daniel 3, but what delights God even more (1 Corinthians 13:3)? Why do you think God values this even more than courage?

Facing our fear head on can feel intensely risky. But it can be a stepping stone to humble faith, renewed confidence, appropriate power and courage, and trusting reverence toward a sovereign, powerful and loving God. "Perfect love casts out fear." It's in the Bible. And it's true.

—Carol Kent
(*Tame Your Fears*, 23)

23. What have you learned from the event described in Daniel 3 that will help you live well as an exile in the world today?

The common excuses for moral and spiritual compromise, especially the blaming of contemporary influences, are contradicted by the faithfulness of these men. In spite of separation from parents and of the corrupting influences of Babylonian religion, political pressure, and immorality, they did not waver in their hour of testing. Critics are probably right that Daniel intended this chapter to remind Israel of the evils of idolatry and the necessity of obeying God rather than men. But the main thrust of the passage is not an invented moral story which actually never happened, as critics infer, but rather a display of a God who is faithful to his people even in captivity and is ever ready to deliver those who put their trust in him.

—John Walvoord
(*Daniel*, 94)

Lessons from a Tree

Daniel 4

OPTIONAL

Memorize Proverbs 6:16–19

There are six things the LORD hates,
    seven that are detestable to him:
        haughty eyes,
        a lying tongue,
        hands that shed innocent blood,
        a heart that devises wicked schemes,
        feet that are quick to rush into evil,
        a false witness who pours out lies
        and a person who stirs up conflict in the community.

In your opinion, what is the worst sin? Some might say sin that morally ravages our relationships and families. For others, murder, theft, or lying is at the top. Many might answer out of the damage they have experienced in their own lives. I would agree that all these sins are grave. But, in my opinion, the root of all sins, the sin that plagues believers more than any other, the trickiest sin, is the sin of pride.

What is pride? It's taking credit for what rightfully belongs to God. It's basking in your own glory when the glory should be given to the Lord. For what do we have or what have we done that was not sourced in him? Pride distorts our thinking and demolishes our gratitude. Pride interferes with our intimacy with God, makes prayer unnecessary, and deforms our judgment. Pride fosters an independent spirit that insists we don't really need God. Pride ultimately opens the door to other sins with their damaging effects.

And pride is easy to hide. Most of us know, as Christians, we aren't supposed to be arrogant, so we bury it under a blanket of false humility or secrecy. We say things like, "Oh, thanks, but it wasn't me," or "You should have given this award to Sally. She's the one who really deserves it," when we are thinking, "It's about time you recognized me for the great job I'm doing." Passages in both the Old and New Testaments back up my claim, and chapter 4 in the book of Daniel should sober us when we feel the tentacles of pride choking us.

Note: King Nebuchadnezzar writes in first person in 4:1–18 and 34–37. The middle portion of the chapter was probably written by Daniel.

This chapter is the only text in the Bible written by a pagan king. It's a letter that Nebuchadnezzer wrote to be distributed throughout his vast kingdom. He ruled forty-three years, from 605 to 562 B.C., and he probably composed the letter near the end of his reign. If so, then over thirty years have passed since Daniel interpreted the king's first dream, and Daniel is now about fifty years old. Although the letter is over twenty-five hundred years old, the insights we can glean are just as valuable today. Ask God to reveal any secret pride in your life and help you change arrogant thinking and behavior. Expect your flesh to resist. Fight for authenticity and humility because it fills God's nostrils with a pleasant aroma. Other people will smell it too, and it will make you beautiful.

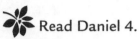 Read Daniel 4.

1. What reasons does the king give for writing about his experience (4:2, 17)?

Pride goes before destruction, a haughty spirit before a fall.
—Proverbs 16:18

2. How was the king feeling about himself and his empire (4:4)?

3. What disturbed his peaceful life (4:5)? What did he do to gain insight (4:6–9)?

4. By now, Daniel had served the king for many years. What can you learn about their relationship from 4:8–9, 18–19?

In Old Testament times, the Holy Spirit did not indwell Old Testament believers as he does New Testament believers today. However, Daniel was particularly blessed by God and enjoyed the privilege of experiencing the Holy Spirit living within him and working through him on a continuous basis. As a result, Nebuchadnezzar sensed that the "spirit of the holy gods" lived in Daniel.

5. As people get to know you, what do you think they sense about you? If you are to be an effective witness for God while living as an exile in an ungodly world, what qualities must your life exhibit?

6. Today, how can we experience God's Spirit living within and through us (1 John 5:10–13; 1 Corinthians 6:19; Romans 8:9–11)?

7. Briefly describe the king's dream (4:10–16).

In Daniel 4:16, we learn that the king's insanity will last for "seven times." The word for *times* is *iddanin* and it is repeated in verses 23, 25, and 32. *Seven* is the biblical number for completion and *times* is interpreted by almost all scholars as *years*. The term can also mean *seasons*, which supports that idea of years, or passing through one round of seasons, which equal one year.

Daniel 4 tells about an ancient tree-hugger—Nebuchadnezzar. He not only dreamed about large trees; he also spent a lot of his time and money working with them. Ancient manuscripts tell us about his love for the cedar forests of Lebanon, his favorite place in the empire outside of Babylon itself. He imported beautiful cedar logs for the decoration of Babylonian buildings, and in the great metropolis of Babylon, he stored immense quantities of grain harvested from plants all across the empire. The city itself was decorated not only with magnificent buildings but also with great vegetation in a huge variety of sizes and shapes.
—Kenneth O. Gangel
(*Daniel*, 91)

DIGGING DEEPER

Jesus' disciples struggled with pride, illustrated in an account recorded by Matthew in his gospel. Study Matthew 20:20–28 and record what happened. How does Jesus define greatness in this story?

Be devoted to one another in love. Honor one another above yourselves.

—Romans 12:10

8. Briefly, describe Daniel's interpretation of the dream (4:20–26).

9. Why was God going to deal with Nebuchadnezzar this way, as foretold in the dream (4:25)?

10. Nebuchadnezzar took personal credit for accomplishing things God gave him the opportunity and means to accomplish. In what areas of your life do you find that it is easy for you to take credit instead of giving the credit to God?

11. How do you deal with pride when you find it cropping up in your life?

Intoxicating False Humility and Pride (*5:38 minutes*).
Are we guilty of "acting small"?

12. *Excessive humility, also known as false humility, can be another form of pride. In what sense might this statement be true?*

13. What did Daniel suggest to the king that might delay or ease God's judgment on his life (4:27)?

14. How much time did God give the king to repent between the dream and the time of its fulfillment (4:29)? What clues in verse 30 reveal that the king had not taken the dream or Daniel's suggestions seriously?

Let another praise you...a stranger, and not your own lips [Proverbs 27:2]. Meaning what? Meaning no self-reference to some enviable accomplishment. Meaning no desire to manipulate and manufacture praise. Meaning authentic surprise when applauded. Genuine, rare humility—regardless. Like the inimitable Principal Cairns, headmaster of an English school, who was walking onto the platform in a line of dignitaries. As he stepped up, a burst of spontaneous applause arose from the audience as an expression of their appreciation. In characteristic modesty, Cairns stepped back to let the man behind pass by as he began to applaud his colleague. He genuinely assumed the applause was for another.
—Charles R. Swindoll
(*Home*, 32–33)

The purpose of this illness is made plain: it is to bring low one who has forgotten his human dependence on *the Most High*, whose prerogative it is to decide who is to receive the right to rule.

—Joyce G. Baldwin
(*Daniel*, 125)

15. Briefly, what happened to the king as he was walking on the roof of his royal palace (4:31–33)?

16. At the end of the seven-year period, what did the king do (4:34)? How had he changed?

17. Have you ever experienced a difficult or humbling situation that brought you into a better relationship with God? If so, and it is not too personal, please share.

18. What happened to the king after God restored his sanity (4:36)?

19. Trace the king's responses to God's work in his life in the following verses. How does his concept of God change as time progresses? Where do you think he stands spiritually at the end of chapter 4? Support your answer. (Scholars disagree over whether or not the king actually came to faith.)

2:46–48

3:28–29

4:1–3

4:34–35, 37

My Father, so seldom do I feel the rich and unshakable peace of heaven, which you promised to me. Is it because I am so often concerned with pleasing others—afraid they'll think poorly of me? Do I work too hard, as if it's my job to make certain people happy? Am I living outside your kingdom of peace, Father, because I'm serving the wrong master?
—prayer of Amy Carmichael, missionary to India
(*You Are My Hiding Place*, 37)

20. What have you learned from the king's letter? List two principles that you intend to apply in your life this week. Remember to renounce the pride of believing that you can accomplish these things in your own strength.

21. How might this incident prepare you to represent Christ well in a post-Christian culture? Why do you think Daniel included the king's letter in his memoirs?

Deciphering the Writing on the Wall

Daniel 5

OPTIONAL

Memorize Galatians 6:1
Brothers and sisters, if someone is caught in a sin, you who live by the Spirit should restore that person gently. But watch yourselves, or you also may be tempted.

Blasphemy is lacking reverence or insulting God. It's also showing contempt for what he values in actions or speech. To our anything-goes culture, very little qualifies as blasphemy anymore. If it draws a laugh, it's not out of bounds. If it mocks God or good people, all the better. If it ridicules people who disagree with us, great. The more outrageous the humiliation, the louder the sneers, and anyone who doesn't join in is prudish, intolerant, and behind the times.

Immersed in a sea of cultural blasphemy, it's easy for us to succumb to the proverbial frog in the pot syndrome—as the heat gently builds, we are boiled to death without knowing it. As God looks down on our world today, what qualifies as blasphemy in his eyes? And how are believers to respond to blasphemers today? These are key questions in our lesson this week.

As you delve into chapter 5, you will probably recognize some similarities with earlier accounts. We find ourselves in a royal court setting again with a foreign monarch who needs help, and Daniel coming to the rescue as the wise man who makes the home-grown magicians look stupid and God look good. But the outcome of this account is eerily different, promising important insight for those who take the time to look carefully and think deeply.

Twenty-three years have passed since the events in the last chapter. Daniel is now about eighty years old. He has served Babylon for sixty years and is probably semiretired. Nebuchadnezzar has died and his son Nabonidus is formally king, except that he hasn't resided in the palace for over ten years. He's off fighting in the army, and his son Belshazzar is ruling in his place. Babylon is losing its grip as the ruling empire over the then-known world, and the armies of Medo-Persia are closing in to take its place.

Our story unfolds on the eve of the fall of the Babylonian Empire, 539 B.C.. Their enemies have blocked the water flow into the supposed impregnable city and they are marching in by way of the waterbed. The scene opens in the throne room of King Belshazzar.

In Daniel 5:2, Nebuchadnezzar is identified as Belshazzar's father but a better translation is ancestor or predecessor. This is because in neither Hebrew nor Aramaic is there a term for grandfather or grandson. Sons and grandsons would call their fathers and their grandfathers *father*.

DIGGING DEEPER

What details concerning the fall of the Babylonian Empire had been predicted long before they came to pass (Jeremiah 51 and 27)? Consult a Bible dictionary for more insight into this significant event in ancient history.

 Read Daniel 5.

1. As Babylon's enemies advance into the capital city, how does the king respond (5:1)?

2. As the evening wears on, what does the king do to liven up the party (5:2–3; see 1:1–2 for background)?

3. Read Exodus 30:22–29, where the Israelites are instructed to make sacred anointing oil as part of their worship in the tabernacle. What are they to do with the oil and how does God view the gold and silver goblets and articles taken from the temple in Jerusalem?

4. To add insult to injury, what did the king and his guests do in Daniel 5:4?

5. What conclusions can you draw about the character of the king?

6. Read 2 Peter 2:10–12, where Peter writes about those who blaspheme God's name in their actions and speech. How might these words apply to King Belshazzar and his guests?

7. The king blasphemed God by his cavalier attitude toward sacred temple articles and using those articles in pagan idol worship. What are some ways people blaspheme God today? See 1 Corinthians 6:18–20 and Ephesians 5:3–4 to get your list started.

Blasphemy is not just defacing a church or a cross. It is a misuse of any part of God's creation. An assault against a fellow human being is an act of blasphemy. After all, we are all created in the image of God (Gen.1:27; James 3:9). An angry word spoken against a fellow believer is an act of blasphemy. After all, Christians are all temples of the Holy Spirit (1 Cor. 3:16). The destruction of the environment for selfish purposes is an act of blasphemy. The land, the air, the seas are each the creation of our holy God.
—Tremper Longman III
(*Daniel*, 152)

DIGGING DEEPER

God does not have a physical body but he sometimes takes on physical attributes to reveal himself to people. What do you learn about the finger of God from the following passages: Exodus 8:19; 31:18; Psalm 8:3?

8. What abruptly occurred to dampen the party atmosphere (Daniel 5:5)? How did the king react (5:6)?

9. The king immediately sent for the wise men of Babylon to read the writing on the wall and to tell him what it meant, but none of them had a clue. Who suggested Daniel be called to help, and why (5:10–12)?

10. Dissect the exchange between the king and Daniel in 5:13–17. What do you think was the tone of their initial conversation?

11. Next, Daniel compared Belshazzar's and Nebuchadnezzar's lives and relationships with God. How were the two kings different (5:18–24)?

12. Finally, Daniel interpreted the words on the wall: MENE, MENE, TEKEL, PARSIN. In a nutshell, what message did God send Belshazzar (5:25–28)?

13. What happened that night to fulfill the writing on the wall (5:30–31)?

14. In what way might the word MENE have application to our lives? See Psalms 39:4–5 and 90:12; and 1 Peter 1:24–25.

DIGGING DEEPER

Compare Belshazzar and the "foolish man" in Luke 12:16–21. What did each man have to take with him into eternity?

15. Knowing what the Bible says about the brevity of life should motivate us to make the most of each day. Specifically what are some things you can do to make every day more meaningful and to be sure your days count for eternity?

16. How might the word TEKEL be applied to our lives? If you were to stand before God today, how would you measure up to his standards?

17. What is the only way to measure up to God's standards (Ephesians 2:4–9)?

18. Why do you think Nebuchadnezzar was returned to his sanity and monarchy (Daniel 4:36–37) while Belshazzar lost both his life and his kingdom (5:30)?

19. The Bible reveals that God is both loving and holy, and his holiness demands that he judge unrighteousness. In his last letter before he was executed, the apostle Paul wrote, "Now there is in store for me the crown of righteousness, which the Lord, *the righteous Judge*, will award to me on that day—and not only to me, but also to all who have longed for his appearing" (2 Timothy 4:8, emphasis added). However, the Bible also says that God's followers are not in a position right now to judge others. In your opinion, why not? What light do the following verses shed on this truth?

God is judge as well as savior, and one must choose which role one will experience from his almighty hand.
—Kenneth O. Gangel
(*Daniel,* 150)

Romans 2:1–4

Matthew 7:1–2

To Judge or Not to Judge (*11:10 minutes*). Let's look at two important questions: Will God judge the world? Should we judge others?

20. What is the difference between judging another person and confronting their sin for the purpose of redemption or restoration? What is the role of a Christian in a world full of blasphemy?

21. What have you learned from Daniel's encounter with King Belshazzar that will help you live well and represent Christ in our post-Christian exile?

How to Survive Conflict When Cats Are After You

Daniel 6

Conflict is part of life because life is full of sinners like you and me. Although we don't mean to, we sometimes disappoint one another. We misunderstand each other. Some of us have not done business with our "junk," and the result is a skewed perspective that can lead to hurtful words and actions, rejection, and foolishness. Many of us fight jealousy which, if unchecked, can easily lead to sin.

If we want to become wise women, we must learn how to respond biblically to conflict. We must take seriously our role as peacemakers and hone our conflict-resolution skills. And if we become proficient peacemakers, one unintended benefit is that we will also prepare ourselves for persecution, should it come our way.

Our brothers and sisters throughout the world are experiencing more persecution than at any other time in world history. If our North American culture continues on its path of entrenched secularism, believers can expect to be ostracized, expelled, and harassed. So whether it's preparation for conflict or persecution, in chapter 6, Daniel will model how to face it with integrity.

Daniel has not changed his location; he is still in the city of Babylon. But Babylon has fallen, and Persia has replaced her as the world's dominant power. Belshazzar is dead and Darius the Mede is in control of the region where Daniel resides.

The exact identity of Darius is still a mystery. Cyrus is king over all of the Persian Empire. His claim to fame is that he allowed the Jewish exiles to return home. Some historians believe that Darius the Mede and Cyrus the Persian are the same man, since Cyrus's father was Persian and his mother was a Mede. He could have used both names to relate to both groups in his empire, depending on where he was. Others think that Darius is governing in Babylon on behalf of Cyrus. For our purposes, this distinction is not particularly important. Darius is in charge and Daniel has again found great favor with a pagan ruler. Our story opens with Darius organizing the local government in that region of the Persian Empire.

 Read Daniel 6.

1. How did Darius set up his government (6:1–2)? What plans did he have for Daniel and why (6:3)?

2. What negative situation did Daniel experience because he distinguished himself with Darius (6:4)? Since the other leaders could not impugn Daniel's integrity, where did they determine he was vulnerable (6:5)?

3. Have you ever distinguished yourself in some way (school, work, ministry, family, sports, or community)? If so, how did you feel about the honor or accomplishment? What positive benefits accompanied this experience? Did any challenges or negative situations result? If you are comfortable, share with the group.

4. What is jealousy? Have you ever heard anyone request prayer to help them overcome their jealousy? Why do you think we seldom talk about our struggles with jealousy?

My friend Brian says that the heart of all human conflict is the phrase "I'm not getting what I want." When you're totally honest about the pain, what's at the center? Could it be that you're not getting what you want? You're getting an invitation to grow, I think, as unwelcome as it may be.
—Shauna Niequist
(*Bittersweet*, 234)

5. What do the following verses reveal about God's view of jealousy?

Proverbs 27:4

Romans 13:13–14

1 Corinthians 3:3

2 Corinthians 12:20

Galatians 5:19–20

....

 Jealousy and Envy (*8:41 minutes*). How can we rid ourselves of these toxic emotions?

....

6. Daniel's rivals devised a scheme to get rid of him. Briefly, what was it (6:6–9)?

7. What was the law of the Medes and Persians and how did it impact our story (6:15)?

8. How did Daniel respond to the newly published edict (6:10)? Daniel was respectful of authority and had earned the trust of the foreign kings by serving them well in the past. What was he risking and why did he defy this edict anyway?

9. What is your initial response to conflict or persecution? Be honest. Why do you think you react this way? What can you learn from Daniel's response?

> When the crises of life threaten us, and our very lives are at stake, calm and quiet dependence on God is our only recourse.
> —Kenneth O. Gangel
> (*Daniel*, 164)

10. Daniel's rivals sprung their trap that very day. What was Daniel praying for when they spied on him (6:11)? In your opinion, why?

11. How did Darius feel when Daniel's rivals told him that Daniel had disobeyed his new law (6:14)?

12. How was Darius trapped by his own decree (6:12–15)?

13. At this point, how much does Darius know about Daniel's God (6:16, 20)?

14. Why did God deliver Daniel according to 6:22–23?

15. How does the author of Hebrews define faith (Hebrews 11:1)?

DIGGING DEEPER

Wring out the great "Hall of Faith" chapter, Hebrews 11. What do you learn about God and faithful men and women?

16. Strong faith is required to handle conflict and persecution well. If you want a faith like Daniel's, how can you go about getting it? Be specific.

DIGGING DEEPER

Jesus instructs believers about how to handle conflict with other believers in three steps (Matthew 18:15–17). What are the three steps and how would they each look in your life and community?

17. After a fretful night, King Darius jumps out of bed and hurries to the pit of lions to find Daniel alive and well. How was the king affected by Daniel's deliverance from the lions (6:23)?

18. What happened to Daniel's rivals (6:24)? What are the lessons for us?

To be successful as a peace-maker, your top priority is to pursue emotional health. Work hard on the inner you.   —Sue

19. What does Darius say in his second decree (6:25–27)? What effect do you think this decree had on the citizens of the vast Persian Empire?

Given the fallen nature of the heart and the complexities of personalities, conflict is unavoidable. How should we deal with our emotions when others are insensitive, manipulative, or just plain mean? Why do men and women tend to deal with conflict differently? To explore these issues, read my book (coauthored with Kelley Mathews) *Leading Women Who Wound.*   —Sue

20. Imagine you are a news reporter assigned to interview Daniel after his experience in the lions' pit. Do you think he will complain to you about being treated unjustly? What do you think Daniel will say? Why?

21. Look back over this episode in Daniel's life. What can you learn from him about how to feel, think, and act in a conflict? Write out as many principles as you can. Which do you need to apply in your life right now to help you hone your peacemaking skills?

A God We Can Count On

Daniel 9

I'm married to a numbers guy, an engineer and computer-aided design professional, who does number puzzles at night to relax. I, on the other hand, did the happy dance the day of my last math class in college, and you will never find me relaxing with a sudoku puzzle. I've never thought of God as a numbers God until I studied Daniel 9. In the first part of the chapter, Daniel records his prayer when he learned that Israel's seventy-year captivity was about to end. Daniel wanted to know exactly when the seventy years would be up. Did those years begin when the first group of captives were taken from their homeland? The second group? The destruction of the temple? What was the starting point? From there, Daniel could determine when God would orchestrate events so that his people could go home.

Yes, God is an exact God. He's the God of science and math and his sovereign plan is calculated down to the cell and second. Seventy years exactly and the Persian king Cyrus would decree that the Israelites could go home. Some did. Some stayed. But God's timetable was precise. We can count on him.

After Daniel records his prayer, he records God's answers, and they are jam-packed with numbers. The answers, rather than focusing only on the time when Israel would be released to go home, laid out the bare bones of Israel's entire future. The last four verses of chapter 9 reveal God's timetable for the Jews and for earth's history. These verses form a framework for other end-time prophecies and are among the most important prophecies in the entire Bible. And these numbers show us that our God is precise, detailed, and accurate. I have a new respect for numbers—and my husband's love for them.

If you are a numbers person, you'll probably love this lesson. If too many numbers make your eyes glaze over, it may be a stretch for you. But persevere. The benefits will be worth the work. I've given you more cues and commentary on the second part of the lesson than usual, to help you through the numerical maze. Understand that scholars don't always agree on what each number means. I'm guiding you using what I believe are sound interpretive methods. Others may not agree, and certainly there is room for respectful dialogue.

In the final analysis, God, in his sovereign precision, has everything under control, down to exact numbers, and that's reassuring, even to this non–numbers girl. Enjoy the journey through God's timetable, and learn what you can. May these realizations strengthen your faith and your respect for the incredible God whom we love and serve.

Prophecy (*6:14 minutes*). What is the significance of prophecy in Scripture, and how can we understand it?

Read Daniel 9:1–19.

1. What spiritual disciplines are obviously part of Daniel's everyday life (9:2–3)? What part do you think these disciplines played in Daniel's stellar character and ability to know how to live well in exile?

2. What part do these disciplines play in your spiritual life and how have they helped you to thrive in exile in our culture today? How can you strengthen these habits? Encourage one another and share ways that have worked for you.

3. Among other passages, Daniel probably read Jeremiah 25:11–12 and 29:10. Daniel had been living in exile in Babylon more than sixty-five years. What questions do you think may have popped into his mind as he was reading?

4. Why did God choose seventy years as the period of time the Israelites would be exiled in Babylon (Leviticus 26:32–35, 43–46; 2 Chronicles 36:15–23)? What else do you learn from these verses regarding Israel's future?

5. What follows Daniel's Bible study is one of the longest and most beautiful prayers in the Bible. The prayer can be divided under three subheads, although certain threads run throughout the whole prayer. Reread and label each portion of the prayer according to the divisions below with a word or phrase characterizing each general section of the prayer.

9:4–11a

The word "love" in the covenant of love in verse 4 is the rich term *hesed*. This refers to the love and affection that God shows his people resulting in his faithfulness and forbearance.

The word "sinned" in verse 5 is the Hebrew word *hata* and it means to miss the mark. For example, Judges 20:16 says that there were seven hundred men who "could sling a stone at a hair and not miss [*hata* (not miss the target)]." Sin is missing God's mark of holy living, a standard that is impossible to meet without an Intercessor who covers our weaknesses and inabilities. Jesus is that Intercessor because he lived a sinless life but took on our sins so that we would not have to pay the penalty we each owe for missing the mark. Old Testament believers' sins were covered when they believed the promises given to their forefathers, and it was counted to them as righteousness (Genesis 15:6).

9:11b–14

9:15–19

6. Specifically, in what ways had the Jews sinned against God that brought on the exile (9:5–6)?

DIGGING DEEPER

One's attitude in prayer is paramount. What do you learn about the proper attitude in prayer that Jesus praises in Luke 18:9–14?

7. When Daniel confessed the sins of the nation, he said, "we have sinned." Why do you think he included himself in the confession?

8. Do you think the nation of Israel really expected to reap God's judgment for their collective sins? Could there be an application here for our nation today? Discuss.

9. In 9:4, Daniel links the act of obeying God to the motivation of love. John reiterates this truth in 1 John 5:2–3. What do these verses say? In your opinion, why is love the greatest motivator, more powerful than either shame or guilt?

> Call to me and I will answer you and tell you great and unsearchable things you do not know.
> —the word of the Lord to Jeremiah (Jeremiah 33:3)

10. After reading the book of Jeremiah, what does Daniel petition God to do? On what basis does he appeal to God (Daniel 9:15–19)?

Biblical prayers serve as beautiful models for us today. Choose one or all of these model prayers to learn more about components of prayer and prayerful attitudes to emulate today: Hannah's prayer in 1 Samuel 2:1–11, Nehemiah's prayer in Nehemiah 1, Jeremiah's prayer in Jeremiah 32:17–25, Mary's prayer in Luke 1:46–55, Jesus' prayer in Luke 11:1–13, and Paul's prayers in Ephesians 1:15–22 and 3:14–21.

When God's people are mystified by the wonders of his word and his work in the world, the best recourse is always prayer—and sometimes the answer will astound you.
—Kenneth O. Gangel
(*Daniel*, 246)

The time of the evening sacrifice would have been at 3 p.m., even though the Jerusalem temple laid in ruins and sacrifices were not offered during the exile. Nevertheless, devout Jews still prayed regularly at these set-aside times.

The phrase *seventy sevens* in verse 24 literally means seventy units of seven. But in the Bible this term "seven" can refer to seven days or seven years. We must attempt to discern which meaning fits the context of this passage. Most scholars believe that a "seven" here represents seven years. Why? Because Daniel had been thinking of God's program for Israel in terms of years. He had just read Jeremiah's prophecy that the exile would last seventy years. Thus, it would have been reasonable for him to interpret these sevens as years. Also, the first sixty-nine sevens are about fulfilled events that show us that Gabriel is talking about years. In addition, the last half of the seventieth seven is described elsewhere as consisting of 3½ years, or 42 months, or 1,260 days. Therefore, most conservative scholars believe this phrase *seventy sevens* means 490 years.

11. After analyzing Daniel's prayer, make a list of lessons you can apply to your own prayer life.

❋ **Read Daniel 9:20–27.**

12. What happened while Daniel was praying? How did God answer his prayer? What was the mandate? (9:20–23)

13. God's answer through Gabriel's words is recorded in 9:24–27, verses jam-packed with numbers and mystery. We will attempt to decipher all we can verse by verse, with the help of scholarly commentators. When a blank is provided, attempt to fill it in; the first one has been done for you. I have provided notes and sidebars that are, in my opinion, the best thinking of respected scholars. Other points of view exist. Try not to get bogged down in the details. Look for the big picture as you dissect the prophecy verse by verse.

Verse 24. This verse identifies God's goals in his salvation plan to redeem the earth and those people who will seek and follow him.

Seventy sevens [490 years] are decreed for your people

[_____] and your holy city [_____] to . . .

1) _____

2) _____

3) _____

4) _____

5) _____

6) _____

a.   What group of people does this prophecy particularly apply to?

b.   These six items represent two sets of three. How are the first three items similar? How about the last three items? In your opinion, which have been accomplished? Which remain to be accomplished?

c. Describe a world where these goals are accomplished.

Count off seven sabbath years—seven times seven years—so that the seven sabbath years amount to a period of forty-nine years.
—Leviticus 25:8

We must remember that Daniel's prayer for forgiveness and restoration was motivated by his reading of Jeremiah's prophecy that the Exile would last seventy years. . . . Gabriel apparently suggests that the end of the seventy-year exile begins a process, one that will last for seventy "sevens" or weeks of years—usually understood as 490 years.
—Tremper Longman III
(*Daniel*, 226)

The meaning of the sixth goal "to anoint the most holy" is debated. We are not sure if this refers to a building, a person, or a group. Archer suggests: "This is not likely a reference to the anointing of Christ because [this Hebrew expression] nowhere else in Scripture refers to a person. Here the anointing of the most holy likely refers to the consecration of the temple of the Lord, quite conceivably the millennial temple, to which so much attention is given in Ezekiel 40–44" (Archer, "Daniel," 113).

These are six broad goals that God intends to accomplish during his salvation plan for the earth.

Some hints are given related to the timing of God's plan in the *seventy sevens*, which equal 490 years. However, some of these goals have not been accomplished. This leads us to believe that there is a gap in the timeline, probably between verse 26 and 27. The reason for this gap will be explained later.

Verse 25. Several important historical events are described in verse 25. These events occurred during the first 483 years, as prophesied in the vision.

Know and understand this:

From the time the word goes out [the issuing of the decree] to restore and rebuild Jerusalem

until the Anointed One, the ruler, comes,

there will be seven "sevens" [49 years], and sixty-two "sevens" [434 years].

[49 + 434 = _____ years total]

It will be rebuilt with streets and a trench, but in times of trouble.

a. First we must discern the beginning point of the prophecy. According to verse 25, what is the beginning point?

There are several decrees issued by kings around this time to rebuild the Jewish temple, but only one decree to rebuild the city of Jerusalem. This was the decree by the Persian monarch Artexerxes given to Nehemiah authorizing him to rebuild Jerusalem. Read Nehemiah 2:1–8 to learn more. The date was approximately 445 B.C., starting the clock running on the prophecy.

The 490 period is divided into three segments; (a) 7 "sevens" (49 years), (b) 62 "sevens" (434 years), and (c) 1 "seven" (7 years). The first period of 49 years may refer to the time in which the rebuilding of the city of Jerusalem, permitted by Artexerxes' decree, was completed (444–395 B.C.). Though Nehemiah's wall construction project took only 52 days, many years may have been needed to remove the city's debris (after being desolate for many decades), to build adequate housing, and to rebuild the streets and a trench.
—J. Dwight Pentecost
(*Bible Knowledge Commentary*, 1363)

b. Next we must discern the ending point of this part of the prophecy. Who do you think the Anointed One might be in verse 25?

Scholars differ on exactly what occurred 483 years after the decree to rebuild Jerusalem. Some insist it was Jesus' crucifixion, others say his triumphal entry. What we do know is that after we consider the variations in different kinds of ancient calendars, the time does fall within the earthly ministry of Jesus of Nazareth! Therefore Jesus is the Anointed One fulfilling all Old Testament prophecies that a King would come out of Israel to save the whole world from their sins and to accomplish the salvation plan set forth by God the Father.

c. What do you think Gabriel is referring to when he talks about something that will be rebuilt with streets and a trench?

Most scholars naturally assume that Gabriel is referring to Jerusalem, but what about the moat? A moat was never constructed around Jerusalem. However, the Kidron and Hinnom valleys on the east, south, and west of the city can function like a moat when rains are heavy.

Verse 26. The events between the sixty-ninth seven, 483 years, and the seventieth seven, 7 years, are marked by turbulence and devastation.

After the sixty-two "sevens,"

the Anointed One [_____] will be put to death

and will have nothing.

The people of the ruler [the Roman general Titus and

his army] **who will come will destroy the city and the**

sanctuary. The end will come like a flood: War will

continue until the end, and desolations have been

decreed.

In the first part of verse 26, the death of Christ is in view and when one does the math, we find that the end of his earthly life occurred at the end of the sixty-ninth week (483 years after the decree to rebuild Jerusalem) but before the last seven years of this earth's history, the seventieth seven. Most scholars believe that when Christ died, the clock stopped for Israel, at verse 26, and the time between verses 26 and 27 is the Church Age, a time when Israel has been set aside for an undesignated period of time. The final week or seven years is needed to complete the entire prophecy.

a. When will God restart his time clock and finish out the final seven-year period on earth (Romans 11:25)?

DIGGING DEEPER

To learn more about what resulted because of the Jews' failure to recognize and accept Christ as their Messiah, read Romans 11:7–12.

The Roman general Titus came with his armies to destroy Jerusalem and the Jewish temple in 70 A.D., approximately forty years after Jesus' crucifixion. Because the Jews failed to recognize their Messiah they lost their homeland and were scattered all over the world for almost two thousand years.

b. How do you feel as you read the prediction in the last part of verse 26? As you consider world events, does it seem this prophecy is being fulfilled?

Because the final emphasis of verse 26 relates to end times, some scholars believe that the Roman General Titus is a prototype of the future leader Antichrist revealed in verse 27.

Verse 27. This verse refers to the final period of earth's history, the last seven years.

DIGGING DEEPER

We learn more about the Antichrist of verse 27 in 2 Thessalonians 2:1–12. What details does Paul give us about this evil leader? In what ways do these two passages confirm one another?

He will confirm a covenant with many for one

"seven" [7 years].

In the middle of the "seven" he will put an end to

sacrifice and offering.

And at the temple he will set up an abomination that causes desolation,

until the end that is decreed is poured out on him.

DIGGING DEEPER

What will happen in the middle of the seven years according to Daniel 2:34–35 and 44–45, Zechariah 14:1–9, and Mark 13:24–27?

The person referred to in verse 27 cannot be the Roman General Titus who destroyed Jerusalem in 70 A.D. because he never made a covenant with the Jewish people. Most conservative scholars believe he is the Antichrist, and the seven years prophesied here are the tribulation described in the book of Revelation. We will learn more about the Antichrist in our last lesson.

This part of the prophecy confirms that at the beginning of the last seven-year period of earth history, the Jews will enter into a treaty with the Antichrist. He will guarantee their safety. Feeling secure, the Jews will rebuild their temple and begin to worship there again. But the Antichrist will soon turn on the Jews and their safety will be short-lived.

Again, we observe that there is a huge time gap between verse 26 when Jerusalem is destroyed in 70 A.D. and verse 27 when the temple has been rebuilt and the sacrificial system is up and running again. This time gap is the period of time that we live in now. No one except God the Father knows when that time gap will end and the clock for Israel will start ticking again. Other prophecies tell us that during this final seven-year period, many Jews will recognize Jesus as their true Messiah, but it will take the events of the tribulation to soften their hearts.

14. Daniel prayed for insight concerning when the Jews would be free to return home to Israel from exile. God answered above and beyond his request by revealing a timetable that began with the decree to free the Jews in Persia and ended with their ultimate deliverance by their long-awaited Messiah and the ushering in of his kingdom. What have you learned about the character of God and his dealing with those he loves from this chapter?

15. We must not forget that God was responding to Daniel as he prayed for insight and understanding so that he could live a holy life and minister to his people. Six hundred years after Daniel's prayer, the Thessalonian Christians asked for more insight into God's timetable for time and eternity. Read 1 Thessalonians 5:1–11. How did Paul instruct the Thessalonians to respond to his teaching on end times? How does God want us to respond to his revelations? What is their ultimate purpose?

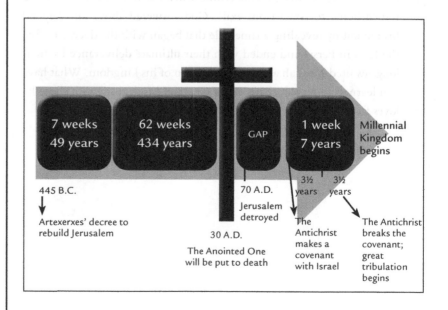

7 weeks
49 years

62 weeks
434 years

GAP

1 week
7 years

Millennial Kingdom begins

3½ years   3½ years

445 B.C.
Artexerxes' decree to rebuild Jerusalem

70 A.D.
Jerusalem detroyed

30 A.D.
The Anointed One will be put to death

The Antichrist makes a covenant with Israel

The Antichrist breaks the covenant; great tribulation begins

A Peek into the Unseen Reality

LESSON 8

Daniel 10

Near the end of my senior year in college, my life crumbled and broke apart. My father was dying, in the last stages of stomach cancer. My mother, always emotionally distant, bitter, and mean-spirited, withdrew and lashed out even more. A four-year romance deteriorated into chaos and confusion. Graduation loomed and my mother's insistence that I study journalism now meant I had to seek employment in a field where I was not a fit. And I had loved the camaraderie of college life, but now my friends were preparing to fan out in a thousand different directions.

I knew God existed, I prayed often, but without a sure decision to follow him, a supportive spiritual family, or any biblical wisdom to guide me, I was an emotional and spiritual wreck. Many days a dark depression overwhelmed me, and when it did, I retreated to our campus chapel. This chapel resembled a small European-style church, with rich wooden pews, velvet tapestries, stained glass windows, and a side garden punctuated with stepping stones, high walls of cascading vines, a rainbow of fragrant blossoms, and a bubbling fountain. Serene and silent, it was my private haven, a place of beauty to run to when I needed to escape from the distresses of the day.

One afternoon, when the burdens seemed particularly heavy, and my sorrows deeper than usual, I sat all afternoon in that chapel and wept, my heart and mind drowning in absolute despair. I remember praying, asking God to take my life, that I didn't want to live anymore. But as I sank deeper and deeper into a chasm of hopelessness, suddenly I heard a strong booming voice—I actually heard this voice audibly. It came from above me and it was loud, but no one was visible, and the voice said just one word: *Wait.* Startled and shocked, I sprinted out of the chapel in terror. But as I've looked back, I know the voice was from God, telling me that I was not alone, regardless of how I felt.

I've never shared that experience before. It was private, just between God and me. And maybe I've been afraid people will think I'm crazy. But, as we will see this week in our lesson, God revealed himself to a distraught Daniel. And God can reveal himself to any of us however he chooses.

OPTIONAL

Memorize 1 John 4:2–4

This is how you can recognize the Spirit of God: Every spirit that acknowledges that Jesus Christ has come in the flesh is from God, but every spirit that does not acknowledge Jesus is not from God. This is the spirit of the antichrist, which you have heard is coming and even now is already in the world. You, dear children, are from God and have overcome them, because the one who is in you is greater than the one who is in the world.

Sometimes his voice is a still small voice. Sometimes it booms. Often he speaks silently in the circumstances. But our God knows just what we need when we need it, and he is able to present himself to us as best suits the situation.

Now that we have his Love Letter, the Bible, I don't think he speaks audibly or sends angels as much as he used to when we did not possess the Scriptures. But he can when he deems it good and helpful. In my case, I was desperate for a word of encouragement and strength, and he had mercy and spoke a word that sustained me. Four years later, I heard the gospel, formally placed my faith in God the Father through Jesus, embraced a church community, and began the incredible ministry journey he planned for me. The book of Daniel declares that God is in control and he knows exactly what he is doing—in my life and yours.

But we must persist in seeking God because powerful forces that we can't see are engulfed in a war for our souls. Our lesson this week gives us a peek into that intriguing and mysterious battle. So look intently, glean, and expect great things from God.

Chapters 10, 11, and 12 are a unit that describes the last vision in the book of Daniel. We will dig into the three parts of this vision in lessons 8 and 9. We will divide up the parts as follows:

1. Prelude to the Vision (10:1–11:1)
2. The Vision (11:2–12:3)
3. Final Words to Daniel (12:4–13)

This week we'll tackle Daniel's experiences before he sees the vision, because chapter 10 contains profound lessons for us related to spiritual warfare and God's dealings with his beloved. The year is around 535 B.C. Some of his fellow Israelites have returned home to begin rebuilding their homeland, but Daniel is elderly and stays behind.

....

 Glimpses into Spiritual Warfare (*5:44 minutes*). Have you ever wondered what lies behind the veil that separates us from the realities of cosmic spiritual warfare? Daniel describes what he sees as he peers through a window that is normally a wall.

....

 Read Daniel 10:1–11:1.

1. What was the general topic of the vision that would soon be revealed to Daniel (10:1)?

There are two equal and opposite errors into which our race can fall about the devils. One is to disbelieve in their existence. The other is to believe, and feel an excessive and unhealthy interest in them. They themselves are equally pleased by both errors and hail a materialist or a medium with the same delight.
—C. S. Lewis
(*Screwtape Letters*, 9)

2. What was Daniel's emotional state at this time in his life (10:2–3)? To understand what might have been the cause, read Ezra 4:1–5, 24. Discuss his situation. What can you take away from this discussion?

3. After Daniel prayed and fasted for three weeks, how did God minister to him (10:4–6)?

Compare what Daniel saw with what the apostle John saw in Revelation 1:12–16.

4. How did Daniel respond? How did the men with him respond (10:7–9)?

Hell's legions are terrified of prayer. Satan trembles when he sees the weakest Christian upon his knees.
—John White (*The Fight*, 223)

Who did Daniel see in 10:5–6? Is this the same figure that interacts with Daniel later in the chapter? Scholars disagree. Some believe the Person in 4–6 is a theophany, that this is Jesus appearing in a glorified state. Others think that this figure is an angel, especially in light of the spiritual warfare that follows. My belief is that both Christ and an angel are present in this chapter, because of the likeness of the first figure to the One in Revelation 1 and Ezekiel 1. But don't get sidetracked trying to identify these majestic beings. They are all sent by God the Father for his purposes. Focus on what you can learn about spiritual warfare and God's interaction and ministry to Daniel. —Sue

DIGGING DEEPER

Compare what happened to Daniel in 10:4–9 to Paul's experience on the Damascus road (Acts 9:1–19).

The tormentors and troublemakers of nature offer an interesting analogy to the evil agencies of the spiritual realm. In the plant kingdom, pests, insects, and blight continually harass the farmer. In the animal kingdom, all creatures have their deadly enemy. And the human body is relentlessly attacked by a multitude of bacteria which cause disease and death. Those who hesitate to accept the testimony of Scripture about the reality of demons may thus find both scientific and philosophical corroboration in nature which has been called God's "oldest testament." The natural world vividly illustrates the activity of demonic beings in the spiritual world.
—Merrill F. Unger (*Demons*, 9–10)

DIGGING DEEPER

Study Jude verses 8 and 9 to learn more about the archangel Michael and spiritual warfare.

5. This supernatural appearance seems to have put Daniel into a deep sleep, or possibly a coma (10:9). What awakened Daniel (10:10)? Note that this also occurs in verses 16 and 18. What is the lesson for us?

6. In the following verses (Daniel 10:11–12, 19), underline the angel's words that were meant to encourage and strengthen Daniel in preparation to see and hear the vision. What do you learn about angels from this interaction with Daniel? What do you learn about Daniel that we should emulate today?

He said, "Daniel, you who are highly esteemed, consider

carefully the words I am about to speak to you, and stand up, for

I have now been sent to you." . . .

Then he continued, "Do not be afraid, Daniel. Since the first

day that you set your mind to gain understanding and to humble

yourself before your God, your words were heard, and I have

come in response to them." . . .

"Do not be afraid, you who are highly esteemed," he said.

"Peace! Be strong now; be strong."

7. Wring out the verses below (Daniel 10:13–14; 10:20–11:1), all statements by the angel. What do you learn about spiritual warfare that goes on around us? Who do you think are the princes of Persia? Greece? Daniel's prince?

"But the prince of the Persian kingdom resisted me twenty-one days. Then Michael, one of the chief princes, came to help me, because I was detained there with the king of Persia. Now I have come to explain to you what will happen to your people in the future, for the vision concerns a time yet to come." . . .

So he said, "Do you know why I have come to you? Soon I will return to fight against the prince of Persia, and when I go, the prince of Greece will come; but first I will tell you what is written in the Book of Truth. (No one supports me against them except Michael, your prince. And in the first year of Darius the Mede, I took my stand to support and protect him.)

8. Several times in our study of Daniel we've observed angels carrying out God's work (4:13–17; 6:22; 9:21–23). What were they doing?

Scholars differ concerning whether 11:1 was spoken by the angel or by Daniel, whose support of Darius (Cyrus) may have contributed to his decree that the Jews could return home after seventy years in exile.

The heavenly warfare is to be directed against first Persia and then Greece, because each of these in turn will have power over God's people.
—Joyce G. Baldwin
(*Daniel*, 202)

There is much we cannot understand about Satan and why God permits him to work. Our minds are limited, and many of these questions will only be answered when we get to heaven.
—Billy Graham ("Why Does God Permit Satan to Exist?")

The crux of my interaction with people has been to expose the insidious reality of Satan's relentless assault of deception on the Christian's mind. He knows that if he can keep you from understanding who you are in Christ, he can keep you from experiencing the maturity and freedom which is your inheritance as a child of God.
—Neil T. Anderson
(*Victory Over the Darkness*, 10)

9. What do you learn about the activities of angels from the following verses?

Psalm 34:7

Matthew 18:10

Hebrews 1:14

Many years ago when I was in seminary a national convention of spirit mediums was being held in the city of Dallas. At this convention mediums were contacting their controls, demons with whom they had contact, to bring messages to individuals. Six of us decided we would attend the meeting, which was announced as being open to the public. We walked into the darkened auditorium and quietly sat down in the rear to observe. The convention was called to order and the chairman of the meeting introduced different mediums who summoned their controls, the demons with whom they were on familiar terms. One after another attempted to make contact and failed, and sat down. Each announced that something was interfering with his making contact. . . . The chairman got up. . . . He pointed to us and said that that row of fellows back there was preventing them from establishing contact. Before they could go on, we were asked to leave. . . . The presence of the Spirit of God in the six believers prevented a manifestation of Satanic power.

—J. Dwight Pentecost (*Your Adversary the Devil*, 181–82)

10. What do you find most interesting about angels and why?

11. Chapter 10 gives us a look at the spiritual warfare going on behind the events in human history. Today Satan's forces still try to hinder God's work in the world. From the following passages, name some of the ways.

2 Corinthians 4:4; Matthew 13:19

1 Timothy 4:1; 2 Corinthians 11:13–15

Job 1:6–12; Luke 22:31

1 Thessalonians 2:18

12. Why is it helpful to know that there are satanic forces at work today?

For our struggle is not against flesh and blood, but against the rulers, against the authorities, against the powers of this dark world and against the spiritual forces of evil in the heavenly realms.
—Ephesians 6:12

13. How do you feel as you consider the unseen realm of spiritual warfare? What do you think is a healthy way to think about these realities?

Paul's letter to the Ephesians ends with instructions on how to live well in the midst of spiritual warfare (Ephesians 6:10–18). Dissect this passage. What do you learn?

As Christians, what should be our reaction to the invasion of the occult and increase in the demonic? We must know the truth about the occult and the spirit world to combat erroneous and increasingly popular views. We must recognize the titanic struggle carried on every day between the forces of darkness and the forces of light. Christians need perspective, lest we belittle the enemies of righteousness, or lest we give them more than their due. We need to be confident of the truth and life we have in Christ and His Word. Neither should we, while investigating Satan and demons, forget the great power and activities of God's angels who remain holy and true to Him and who resist Satan and his angels. Christians must have an answer for a needy and confused world.

—C. Fred Dickason
(*Angels, Elect and Evil*, 11)

14. Can you think of a time when one of God's angels may have been at work in your life? In the lives of others you know? Please share if you are comfortable.

The End; He Wins

Daniel 11–12

My purpose in the Discover Together Series is to take you through the biblical text, usually verse by verse, using sound self-discovery methods that help the passages stick in your mind and heart so they are cherished and applied in your life. In my experience, God often uses this approach to help us grow into mature, godly women, ready to tackle life's challenges. That transformation is my goal. But as we conclude our study in Daniel, instead of our usual format, I've prayerfully decided to provide you with a summary of verses two through thirty-five rather than taking you verse by verse through the first portion of the vision.

These verses contain *fulfilled* prophecy about the rule of unnamed kings and their reigns from before Christ's first advent. This first part of the vision is long, tedious, and difficult to follow. This prophecy recorded the historical period from the Persian Empire to the time of Antiochus Epiphanes, and especially how these events would impact Israel. As such, it has little relevance for us today.

These verses were of tremendous interest to Daniel and Jews who lived before the first coming of Christ, of course. They learned that the Persian Empire would fall to the great Greek general Alexander the Great, and Alexander would be overtaken by the Seleucids (Syria) and the Ptolemies (Egypt). They, like us, needed to know that God continued to be in control of the events of history, regardless of how overwhelming and discouraging their circumstances. But to those of us living in the third millennium after Christ, the latter parts of the vision are far more relevant and meaningful. To you history buffs who are disappointed that we are not covering the first part of the vision in detail, I'm providing several resources to guide you in a sidebar—definitely a *digging deeper* assignment. For others, the brief overview I supply here and in several sidebars should suffice.

In the prior lesson, we studied Daniel's experiences before the angel appeared to him and we were privileged to peek into the unseen world of spiritual warfare. In this lesson, we will focus on the second part of the

OPTIONAL

Memorize Isaiah 40:10–11

See, the Sovereign LORD comes with power, and he rules with a mighty arm. See, his reward is with him, and his recompense accompanies him. He tends his flock like a shepherd: He gathers the lambs in his arms and carries them close to his heart; he gently leads those that have young.

For an easy-to-understand explanation of the first part of the prophecy in Daniel 11:2–35, go to www.sonic light.com, click on Dr. Tom Constable's notes on Daniel and read pages 125 to 135. Another interesting source is *Daniel*, Holman Old Testament Commentary by Kenneth Gangel. Read pages 297 to 304. You'll find these accounts as full of intrigue and drama as any modern day soap opera.

The first part of the vision in chapter 11 contains approximately 135 prophecies, all now fulfilled as predicted, proving God's ability to anticipate history by hundreds of years. What a grand introduction to the prophecies that are still future for us! On days when you are tempted to doubt that God has control of everything, consider this truth and take heart. —Sue

The term *god of fortresses* in 11:38 suggests that the Antichrist puts his trust in military power.

vision which reveals end-time prophecy. The Antichrist is the main character in this fascinating, unfolding saga. Then we will close out our study by examining a dialogue between Daniel and two heavenly beings. Get ready for a look into God's culminating plan for our planet!

Read Daniel 11:36–45.

1. These verses do not seem to have been fulfilled by Antiochus, the ancient ruler described in the first part of the vision. This section is thought to be future prophecy, a description of the evil ruler in the end times, the Antichrist, who is foreshadowed by Antiochus. What do you learn about his character from verses 36–37?

Commentators disagree about the meaning of the phrase "He will show no regard . . . for the one desired by women" (11:37). Some explain it as a reference to goddess worship. Others wonder if it might refer to Jesus. Certainly many women were drawn to him as Savior and Lord through the centuries.

2. What can you learn about the Antichrist's sense of values from 11:38?

3. What can you learn about his dealings with others from 11:39?

4. A great war is described in 11:40. What words reveal that initially the Antichrist has the upper hand?

5. Once the Antichrist has defeated enemies from the North and enemies from the South, whom will he target (11:41–44)?

6. After great military success, where will he set up headquarters (11:45)?

DIGGING DEEPER

The New Testament speaks of the Antichrist as *the man of lawlessness* in 2 Thessalonians 2:1–10. What similarities can you find between this *man of lawlessness* in 2 Thessalonians and the angel's revelation about the Antichrist in Daniel 11:36–45? What additional insight can you glean from a Bible dictionary?

The first portion of the vision centers on the affairs of two kingdoms whose kings he called "the king of the South" and "the king of the North." These north and south directions are in relation to Israel, the land of Daniel and his people. The nation to the south was Egypt (v. 8), which Ptolemy I and his descendants ruled. The kingdom to the north was what later became Syria, which Seleucus I and his heirs governed. The Holy Land stood between these two great powers, Egypt and Syria, and it became territory that each one coveted and tried to possess. Territorial tensions still plague that region of the world.

The break at 11:36 is not apparent at first. Prophecies sometimes jump over centuries without warning, but when we begin to read statements like "He will exalt and magnify himself above every god and will say unheard-of things against the God of gods. He will be successful until the time of wrath is completed . . ." we sense a shift in the magnitude of the prophecy. And when we read "at the time of the end . . ." (verse 40) we can be sure that the prophecy refers to God's culminating plan upon the earth.

The seas mentioned in verse 45 are probably the Mediterranean Sea to the west and the Dead Sea to the east. The "beautiful holy mountain" is likely Mount Zion where the temple stood. (Locate these places in a Bible atlas for a better sense of their location.) Thus Antichrist will probably use the Jerusalem temple as his headquarters.

7. In the first portion of the vision, Antiochus Epiphanes (the king of the North who ruled Syria from 175 to 164 B.C.) violently persecuted the Jews. History confirms this fact. Many scholars believe that Antiochus's treatment of the Jews foreshadows the way the Antichrist will treat them in the future. What can you glean from 11:30–35 concerning this earlier persecution and the Jews' response to it?

8. What do you think enables believers to stand firm in their faith when it would be easiest to compromise or deny God?

9. What spiritual good is often accomplished through persecution or other crisis situations (Daniel 11:35; James 1:2–4; 1 Peter 1:7; 4:1–2)?

10. Share an incident in which a difficult situation ultimately worked out for good.

11. How will the Antichrist meet his end (Daniel 11:45; 2:34–35, 44–45)?

12. What will take place after this last powerful Gentile ruler is crushed (Zechariah 14:9; Zephaniah 3:14–20)?

God is in control in spite of present circumstances. In sixth-century Babylon it looked to the godly as if Babylon and then Persia were in control. But they weren't. In second-century Palestine it looked as if Antiochus Epiphanes was in control, but he wasn't. In the first century of Jesus and Paul, it looked as if Rome was in control, but it wasn't. To Christians living two thousand years after Jesus, it may look as if Satan is in control, but he isn't. God is in control, and because of that we can have boundless joy and optimism in the midst of our struggles.

—Tremper Longman III (*Daniel*, 299)

DIGGING DEEPER

The book of Revelation sheds light on the actions of the Antichrist in the end times where he is referred to as "the beast." What can you learn from Revelation chapters 13 and 17? These prophecies are complex and often confusing. Look for general themes to enhance your understanding.

DIGGING DEEPER

Study Zechariah chapter 14 to learn more about the return of Christ to the earth. These prophecies are full of symbolism and references to the Holy Land and surrounding nations. Look for general themes to enhance your understanding.

 Read Daniel 12:1–4.

DIGGING DEEPER

The angel said that *multitudes who sleep in the dust of the earth will awake* (Daniel 12:2). Paul provided more information about the resurrection of our physical bodies in 1 Corinthians 15:35–58. What details do you learn about this resurrection? Do any of these truths surprise you?

13. Throughout his memoirs, Daniel is particularly concerned about the future of his people, the Jews. What is the ultimate future of Jewish people (12:1–3)? What do you learn that impacts all people of all times everywhere?

14. After dreary news of the dark events that will usher in the end of our earth as we know it, what good news shines forth in 12:3?

In the ancient Near East the custom was to "seal" an important document by impressing upon it the identifying mark of the parties involved and the recording scribe. A sealed text was not to be tampered with or changed. The original document was duplicated and placed ("closed up") in a safe place where it could be preserved.
—Stephen R. Miller
(*Daniel*, 320)

15. What is Daniel instructed to do with the vision (12:4)? What do you think this means?

 **Read Daniel 12:5–13.**

16. The vision concludes in 12:4. Remember that Daniel is still on the bank of the Tigris River. What does he see now (12:5)?

17. What question did one angel pose to the other (12:6)? What was the answer (12:7)? What do you think this means?

The other angel answered in 12:7, "It will be for a time, times and half a time." In Daniel 9:27, we suggested that this expression means three and a half years, exactly one-half of the last seven years of earth's history, also known as the tribulation.

An important purpose of the tribulation will be to break the Jews of their stubborn resistance to Christ, their Messiah. This is probably the meaning of "When the power of the holy people has been finally broken, all these things will be completed" (12:7).

18. Daniel, like many of us, was somewhat confused by all he was learning, so he asked for clarification (12:8). The angel's response (12:9–13) offers helpful counsel not only for Daniel but also for us as we conclude our study. Below, dissect each section. What do you think the angel was communicating to Daniel in these final verses? How might each apply to you?

Verses 9–10

Go your way, Daniel, because the words are rolled up and sealed until the time of the end. Many will be purified, made spotless and refined, but the wicked will continue to be wicked. None of the wicked will understand, but those who are wise will understand.

DIGGING DEEPER

In Romans chapter 11, Paul writes concerning Israel's future. What symbols does he use to express the truth that God loves the Jews and has an ultimate plan for them in his kingdom? How does this text help you understand portions of the vision given to Daniel in chapters 11 and 12?

The angel provides a time-table again, showing us the number of days between the setting up of the pagan image in the temple (in the middle of the tribulation) and the end of the tribulation. But verses 11 and 12 cause as much confusion as clarification because the earlier revelation was 1,260 days, not 1,290 days or 1,335 days. Here we have an additional 30 to 45 days after the tribulation and before Christ sets up the millennial kingdom. What will happen during those days? We don't know for sure. Scholars have suggested possibilities; for example, these days might be set aside for celebration or for judgment. But I think we may be missing the point. The angel pronounced a blessing on those who wait well. I wonder if that's what the angel is emphasizing? These prophecies are mysteries given to encourage us, but we must not obsess about them. Why has God given them to us? I believe God wants us to know something about his great plan of history and end times to help us persevere and live holy lives now. A life of faith is a life of waiting—until he returns. How well do you wait? That's the point!   —Sue

From the time that the daily sacrifice is abolished and the abomination that causes desolation is set up, there will be 1,290 days. Blessed is the one who waits for and reaches the end of the 1,335 days.

Verse 13

As for you, go your way till the end. You will rest, and then at the end of the days you will rise to receive your allotted inheritance.

As Jesus was sitting on the Mount of Olives, the disciples came to him privately. "Tell us," they said, "when will this happen, and what will be the sign of your coming and of the end of the age?"

Jesus answered: "Watch out that no one deceives you. For many will come in my name, claiming, 'I am the Messiah,' and will deceive many. You will hear of wars and rumors of wars, but see to it that you are not alarmed. Such things must happen, but the end is still to come. Nation will rise against nation, and kingdom against kingdom. There will be famines and earthquakes in various places. All these are the beginning of birth pains.
—Matthew 24:3–8

 Puzzle Pieces of Prophecy (*7:21 minutes*). What's the significance of putting together what we learn from the prophecy in Daniel?

19. Think back over your study of Daniel's memoirs, from the time he arrived as an exile in Babylon to his final days looking back on his service to several kings and then forward to God's future plans. What have you learned that can help you live courageously as an exile in our culture?

Every tomorrow has two handles; we can take hold by the handle of anxiety or by the handle of faith.

—*Southern Baptist Brotherhood Journal* (Gangel, *Daniel*, 318)

20. Do you have a favorite account that you think will stay with you and help you stand strong for the Lord in the days ahead?

Thus this great book closes with a reminder that the present age of Gentile domination is not all that God has in store for humankind. There is another age coming, beyond the present one, in which Jesus Christ will reign in righteousness and holiness on the earth (cf. Isa. 11:9; Zech. 9:10). Christians should look forward to the beginning of this Messianic age and pray for its coming (Matt. 6:10; Luke 11:2). Whereas this book would have encouraged the Jews of Daniel's day, it has become increasingly encouraging to God's people as history has unfolded. Today we can see, as never before, how God has fulfilled His predictions exactly in the past. This gives us great confidence as we anticipate His faithfulness to those promises that still remain unfulfilled.

What other practical effects should an understanding of Daniel's prophecies have on us today? We can understand how God will create history; we can know the "times and seasons" that are still future. This knowledge should make us feel the urgency of our commission (Matt. 28:19-20); it should spur us on to evangelism and discipleship. It should also give us a sense of peace as we go through trouble and hope that God will win the battle over evil. It should encourage us to inform God's people of what He has revealed so they can be informed and ready for what is coming. And it should cause us to live holy lives in view of the Lord's return.

21. What do you think you will remember about the book of Daniel a year from now? Five years from now? Ten years from now?

—Thomas L. Constable (*Dr. Constable's Notes on Daniel*)

Works Cited

Anderson, Neil T. *Victory Over the Darkness: Realizing the Power of Your Identity in Christ*. Ventura, CA: Regal Books, 1990.

Archer, Gleason L., Jr. "Daniel." *Daniel and the Minor Prophets*. Vol. 7. *The Expositor's Bible Commentary*. 12 vols. Edited by Frank E. Gaebelein and Richard P. Polcyn. Grand Rapids: Zondervan, 1985.

Baldwin, Joyce G. *Daniel: An Introduction and Commentary*. Tyndale Old Testament Commentaries. Downers Grove, IL: IVP Academic, 1978.

Briscoe, Jill. *God's Name, God's Nature: Knowing God by His Old Testament Names*. Wheaton, IL: Victor Books, 1988.

Carmichael, Amy. *You Are My Hiding Place*. Minneapolis, MN: Bethany House, 1991.

Constable, Thomas L. *Dr. Constable's Notes on Daniel*. 2013. www.soniclight.com. Used by permission.

Dickason, C. Fred. *Angels, Elect and Evil*. Chicago: Moody Publishers, 1975.

Feinberg, Charles. *Daniel: The Kingdom of the Lord*. Winona Lake, IN: BMH Books, 1981.

Gangel, Kenneth O. *Daniel*. Holman Old Testament Commentary. Edited by Max Anders. Nashville: Broadman & Holman, 2001.

Goldingay, John E. *Daniel*. Word Biblical Commentary. Vol. 30. Nashville: Thomas Nelson, 1996.

Graham, Billy. "Why Does God Permit Satan to Exist?" *Arkansas Democrat-Gazette*, February 4, 1992.

Jensen, Irving L. *Ezekiel and Daniel: A Self-Study Guide*. Chicago: Moody Bible Institute, 1968.

Kent, Carol. *Tame Your Fears: And Transform Them into Faith, Confidence, and Action*. Colorado Springs: NavPress, 1993.

Kubler-Ross, Elisabeth. *Death: The Final Stage of Growth*. New York: Touchstone, 1986.

Lewis, C. S. *The Screwtape Letters*. New York: Macmillan, 1948.

Longman, Tremper, III. *Daniel*. The NIV Application Commentary. Grand Rapids: Zondervan, 1999.

Miller, Stephen R. *Daniel*. The New American Commentary. Vol. 18. Nashville: Broadman & Holman, 1994.

Niequist, Shauna. *Bittersweet: Thoughts on Change, Grace, and Learning the Hard Way*. Grand Rapids: Zondervan, 2010.

Packer, J. I. *Knowing God*. Downers Grove, IL: InterVarsity Press, 1973.

Pentecost, J. Dwight. *The Bible Knowledge Commentary: Old Testament*. Edited by John F. Walvoord and Roy B. Zuck. Wheaton, IL: Victor Books, 1985.

————. *Your Adversary the Devil*. Grand Rapids: Zondervan, 1969.

Sande, Ken. *The Peacemaker*. Grand Rapids: Baker, 2004.

Swindoll, Charles R. *Home: Where Life Makes Up Its Mind*. Portland, OR: Multnomah, 1979.

————. *Tale of the Tardy Oxcart*. Nashville: Word Publishing, 1998.

Unger, Merrill F. *Demons in the World Today*. Wheaton, IL: Tyndale, 1971.

Unice, Nicole. *She's Got Issues: Seriously Good News for the Stressed-Out, Secretly Scared Control Freaks Like Us*. Carol Stream, IL: Tyndale, 2012.

Walvoord, John. *Daniel: The Key to Prophetic Revelation*. Chicago: Moody Publishers, 1971.

White, John. *The Fight*. Downers Grove, IL: InterVarsity Press, 1976.

About the Author

S ue Edwards is associate professor of educational ministries and leadership (her specialization is women's studies) at Dallas Theological Seminary, where she has the opportunity to equip men and women for future ministry. She brings over thirty years of experience into the classroom as a Bible teacher, curriculum writer, and overseer of several megachurch women's ministries. As minister to women at Irving Bible Church and director of women's ministry at Prestonwood Baptist Church in Dallas, she has worked with women from all walks of life, ages, and stages. Her passion is to see modern and postmodern women connect, learn from one another, and bond around God's Word. Her Bible studies have ushered thousands of women all over the country and overseas into deeper Scripture study and community experiences.

In addition to her Bible studies, Sue has coauthored several titles: *Organic Mentoring: A Mentor's Guide to Relationships with Next Generation Women* (with Barbara Neumann, Kregel 2014); *Leading Women Who Wound: Strategies for an Effective Ministry* (with Kelley Mathews, Moody 2009); *Mixed Ministry: Working Together as Brothers and Sisters in an Oversexed Society* (with Kelley Mathews and Henry Rogers, Kregel 2008); *Women's Retreats: A Creative Planning Guide* (with Kelley Mathews and Linda Robinson, 2004); and *New Doors in Ministry to Women: A Fresh Model for Transforming Your Church, Campus, or Mission Field* (with Kelley Mathews, Kregel 2003).

Sue has a doctor of ministry degree from Gordon-Conwell Theological Seminary in Boston and a master's in Bible from Dallas Theological Seminary. With Dr. Joye Baker, she oversees the Dallas Theological Seminary doctor of ministry degree in Christian education with a women-in-ministry emphasis.

Sue has been married to David over forty years. They have two married daughters, Heather and Rachel, and five grandchildren. David is a retired CAD applications engineer, a lay prison chaplain, and founder of their church's prison ministry.